**IXL MATH WORKBOOK**

# GRADE 3
# MULTIPLICATION

ISBN: 9781947569270
28 27 26 25 24 4 5 6 7 8

Printed in China

Get ready to multiply! Skip count to find the number of items in each group.

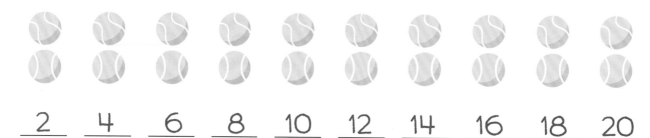

| 2 | 4 | 6 | 8 | 10 | 12 | 14 | 16 | 18 | 20 |

_____  _____  _____  _____  _____  _____

_____  _____  _____  _____  _____  _____

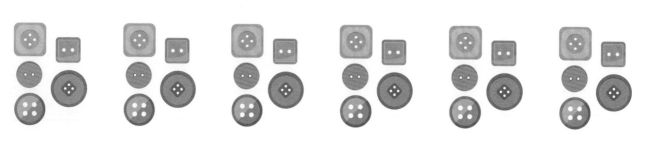

_____  _____  _____  _____  _____  _____

IXL.com
skill ID
LQM

For more practice, visit IXL.com or the IXL mobile app and enter this code in the search bar.

If you have equal groups, you can multiply to find the total! Fill in the blanks. Follow the example.

$\underline{2}$ + $\underline{2}$ + $\underline{2}$ = $\underline{6}$

$\underline{3}$ groups of $\underline{2}$ = $\underline{6}$

$\underline{3}$ × $\underline{2}$ = $\underline{6}$

___ + ___ + ___ = ___

___ groups of ___ = ___

___ × ___ = ___

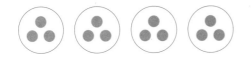

___ + ___ + ___ + ___ = ___

___ groups of ___ = ___

___ × ___ = ___

___ + ___ + ___ = ___

___ groups of ___ = ___

___ × ___ = ___

___ + ___ + ___ + ___ + ___ = ___

___ groups of ___ = ___

___ × ___ = ___

___ + ___ + ___ + ___ + ___ = ___

___ groups of ___ = ___

___ × ___ = ___

**Fill in the blanks.**

How many scoops of ice cream are there?

___ + ___ + ___ = ___

___ groups of ___ = ___

___ × ___ = ___

How many windows do you see?

___ + ___ + ___ = ___

___ groups of ___ = ___

___ × ___ = ___

How many hot-air balloons are there?

___ + ___ + ___ + ___ = ___

___ groups of ___ = ___

___ × ___ = ___

If you have equal rows, you can multiply to find the total. Fill in the blanks.
Follow the example.

$\underline{2}$ rows of $\underline{3}$ = $\underline{6}$

$\underline{2}$ × $\underline{3}$ = $\underline{6}$

___ rows of ___ = ___

___ × ___ = ___

___ rows of ___ = ___

___ × ___ = ___

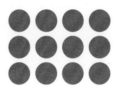

___ rows of ___ = ___

___ × ___ = ___

___ rows of ___ = ___

___ × ___ = ___

___ rows of ___ = ___

___ × ___ = ___

**FLIP IT!** | Look at the first two problems on the page.
One has 2 rows of 3. The other has 3 rows of 2.
Is the total different?

IXL.com
skill ID

HZL

**Fill in the blanks.**

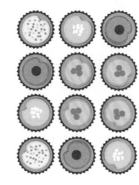

_____ rows of _____ = _____

_____ × _____ = _____

_____ rows of _____ = _____

_____ × _____ = _____

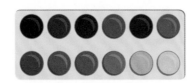

_____ rows of _____ = _____

_____ × _____ = _____

_____ rows of _____ = _____

_____ × _____ = _____

**Fill in the blanks to solve each problem.**

Mr. Walker puts the desks in his classroom in 3 rows. There are 5 desks in each row. How many desks are there in all? Draw a picture to help.

__3__ rows of __5__ = 15

__3__ × __5__ = 15

Alice is wearing 3 bracelets on each arm. How many bracelets is she wearing? Draw a picture to help.

_____ groups of _____ = _____

_____ × _____ = _____

Louis bought 3 bunches of bananas. Each bunch had 4 bananas in it. How many bananas did he buy in all? Draw a picture to help.

_____ bunches of _____ = _____

_____ × _____ = _____

## Let's Learn!

Each number in a multiplication sentence has a special name. The numbers you multiply together are called the **factors**. The result is called the **product**.

$$2 \times 5 = 10$$

factors          product

**Show off your new knowledge! Answer each question.**

In $2 \times 3 = 6$, which number is the product? Which numbers are the factors?

Write a multiplication sentence where the factors are 2 and 4. What is the product?

Write a multiplication sentence where the product is 12 and one of the factors is 3. What is the other factor?

**CHALLENGE YOURSELF!**  Can you write a multiplication sentence where the two factors are the same?

Evan owns a bakery. He uses multiplication every day! Today, Evan needs to make chocolate cupcakes. Each batch of cupcakes calls for 2 eggs. **Multiply by 2 to help Evan find the total number of eggs needed.**

| Batches of cupcakes | Batches × eggs per batch | Total number of eggs |
|---|---|---|
| 1 | 1 × 2 | 2 |
| 2 | 2 × 2 | |
| 3 | 3 × 2 | |
| 4 | 4 × 2 | |
| 5 | 5 × 2 | |
| 6 | 6 × 2 | |
| 7 | 7 × 2 | |
| 8 | 8 × 2 | |
| 9 | 9 × 2 | |
| 10 | 10 × 2 | |

**FIND THE PATTERN!** The numbers you wrote are called **multiples** of 2. How many of them are even? How many are odd? What do you notice about multiples of 2?

**Multiply.**

2 × 4 = _____

2 × 3 = _____

2 × 2 = _____

6 × 2 = _____

4 × 2 = _____

2 × 10 = _____

2 × 7 = _____

2 × 1 = _____

7 × 2 = _____

1 × 2 = _____

2 × 9 = _____

10 × 2 = _____

5 × 2 = _____

2 × 8 = _____

3 × 2 = _____

2 × 6 = _____

9 × 2 = _____

2 × 5 = _____

2 × 2 = _____

8 × 2 = _____

IXL.com
skill ID
94M

**Let's Learn!**

As you discovered on page 9, multiples of 2 and even numbers are the same thing! You can use this rule to tell whether large numbers are multiples of 2.

**Try it yourself! Circle the multiples of 2.**

| | | | |
|---|---|---|---|
| 70 | 85 | 204 | 558 |
| 5,442 | 90,435 | 100,332,438 | 3,942,384,931 |

**Solve each riddle.**

If you multiply me by 2, you get 2. What am I?

I am a multiple of 2, and my digits add to 9. I am less than 20. What am I?

I am a multiple of 2. I am less than 2 × 5 and more than 2 × 3. What am I?

I am a multiple of 2. I am less than 20 and more than 10. My second digit is two times my first digit. What am I?

Multiply.

3 × 1 = _____          3 × 6 = _____

3 × 2 = _____          3 × 7 = _____

3 × 3 = _____          3 × 8 = _____

3 × 4 = _____          3 × 9 = _____

3 × 5 = _____          3 × 10 = _____

| UNLOCK THE SECRET! | Can you find the secret about multiples of 3? Try adding the digits in one of your answers together. What do you get? Have you written that number somewhere else on the page? |

**Let's Learn!**

As you discovered, a number is a multiple of 3 if its digits add up to a multiple of 3. For example, the number 72 is a multiple of 3. You can tell because 7 + 2 = 9, and 9 is a multiple of 3.

**Try it yourself! Circle the multiples of 3.**

63          84          92          105          134          372          902

**Solve each riddle.**

I am a multiple of 3. I am also a multiple of 2. I am more than 10 and less than 15. What am I?

I am a multiple of 3. I am more than 2 × 7 and less than 2 × 8. What am I?

I am a multiple of 3. I am less than 30 and more than 20. My second digit is two times my first digit. What am I?

**Multiply.**

$3 \times 5 = $ _____

$3 \times 10 = $ _____

$2 \times 3 = $ _____

$4 \times 3 = $ _____

$3 \times 6 = $ _____

$5 \times 3 = $ _____

$3 \times 9 = $ _____

$3 \times 4 = $ _____

$10 \times 3 = $ _____

$3 \times 3 = $ _____

$3 \times 3 = $ _____

$9 \times 3 = $ _____

$3 \times 1 = $ _____

$1 \times 3 = $ _____

$7 \times 3 = $ _____

$3 \times 8 = $ _____

$8 \times 3 = $ _____

$3 \times 2 = $ _____

$6 \times 3 = $ _____

$3 \times 7 = $ _____

IXL.com
skill ID
38K

**Answer each question.**

Aaron made 6 origami bookmarks and sold them for $3 each. How much money did he make?

_____

Jessie has 2 piles of comic books. There are 4 comic books in each pile. How many comic books does Jessie have?

_____ comic books

Becca wants to sew colorful patches onto the elbows of her jackets. She has 3 jackets to sew. How many patches does she need?

_____ patches

In Mrs. Taylor's art room, there are small, medium, and large paint brushes. If there are 7 of each size, how many paint brushes are there in all?

_____ paint brushes

**Write the missing numbers.**

$3 \times \underline{\hspace{2em}} = 9$

$2 \times 10 = \underline{\hspace{2em}}$

$3 \times \underline{\hspace{2em}} = 27$

$\underline{\hspace{2em}} \times 5 = 10$

$3 \times \underline{\hspace{2em}} = 6$

$2 \times 6 = \underline{\hspace{2em}}$

$3 \times \underline{\hspace{2em}} = 12$

$\underline{\hspace{2em}} \times 7 = 21$

$\underline{\hspace{2em}} \times 9 = 18$

$3 \times 5 = \underline{\hspace{2em}}$

$2 \times \underline{\hspace{2em}} = 2$

$3 \times \underline{\hspace{2em}} = 30$

$\underline{\hspace{2em}} \times 4 = 8$

$3 \times \underline{\hspace{2em}} = 18$

$2 \times \underline{\hspace{2em}} = 14$

Bruno's Bookstore is having a one-day book sale. Every book is just $4! Lisa wants to know how much it will cost to buy different numbers of books. **Multiply to help her out!**

| Number of books | Books × cost per book | Total cost |
| --- | --- | --- |
| 1 | 1 × $4 | |
| 2 | 2 × $4 | |
| 3 | 3 × $4 | |
| 4 | 4 × $4 | |
| 5 | 5 × $4 | |
| 6 | 6 × $4 | |
| 7 | 7 × $4 | |
| 8 | 8 × $4 | |
| 9 | 9 × $4 | |
| 10 | 10 × $4 | |

**DIG DEEPER!** | Look at the multiples of 4. They are all even. Why do you think that is?

**Multiply.**

4 × 2 = _____          4 × 5 = _____          4 × 6 = _____

10 × 4 = _____         1 × 4 = _____          4 × 10 = _____

4 × 4 = _____          3 × 4 = _____          4 × 1 = _____

4 × 3 = _____          4 × 8 = _____          2 × 4 = _____

5 × 4 = _____          9 × 4 = _____          4 × 7 = _____

8 × 4 = _____          4 × 4 = _____          4 × 9 = _____

7 × 4 = _____          6 × 4 = _____          4 × 8 = _____

IXL.com
skill ID
5U6

**Answer each riddle.**

Which multiple of 4 is equal to 2 × 6?

Which multiple of 4 is less than 3 × 7 but more than 2 × 9?

Which number can you multiply by 4 to get 28?

**Solve the logic puzzle.**

Aaron, Ethan, Mia, Logan, and Grace each have a different favorite number. Use the clues to figure out which number belongs to which person.

Aaron's favorite number is twice as big as Mia's.

Ethan's favorite number is 4 times as big as Logan's.

Grace's favorite number is 3 times as big as Mia's.

| Favorite number | Aaron | Ethan | Mia | Logan | Grace |
|---|---|---|---|---|---|
| 4 | | | | | |
| 5 | | | | | |
| 8 | | | | | |
| 12 | | | | | |
| 20 | | | | | |

**Multiply.**

5 × 5 = _____

3 × 5 = _____

2 × 5 = _____

5 × 7 = _____

5 × 1 = _____

9 × 5 = _____

4 × 5 = _____

1 × 5 = _____

7 × 5 = _____

10 × 5 = _____

5 × 9 = _____

5 × 5 = _____

5 × 6 = _____

5 × 8 = _____

5 × 3 = _____

5 × 2 = _____

6 × 5 = _____

5 × 4 = _____

5 × 10 = _____

8 × 5 = _____

**LOOK AGAIN!** What do you notice about the last digit of each multiple of 5?

**Multiply to find out how much the coins are worth.**

___8___ × 5 cents = ___40___ cents

In Japan, each of these coins is worth 5 yen.

_____ × 5 yen = _____ yen

In India, each of these coins is worth 5 rupees.

_____ × 5 rupees = _____ rupees

In Britain, each of these coins is worth 5 pence.

_____ × 5 pence = _____ pence

**Let's Learn!**

If a number ends in 5 or 0, it's a multiple of 5! You can use that rule to figure out whether large numbers are multiples of 5.

**Try it yourself! Circle all the multiples of 5.**

| 90 | 159 | 355 | 4,230 | 36,504 | 759,205 |
|----|-----|-----|-------|--------|---------|

**Write the missing numbers.**

$4 \times 8 =$ _____

$5 \times$ _____ $= 10$

$4 \times 3 =$ _____

$5 \times$ _____ $= 30$

$7 \times$ _____ $= 28$

_____ $\times 9 = 45$

_____ $\times 5 = 5$

_____ $\times 4 = 16$

$5 \times$ _____ $= 15$

_____ $\times 5 = 20$

$8 \times$ _____ $= 40$

_____ $\times 5 = 50$

_____ $\times 2 = 8$

_____ $\times 4 = 36$

$5 \times$ _____ $= 35$

**Answer each question.**

Basketball games are played with 2 teams of 5 players each. How many players is that in all?

_____ players

Peter just signed up for a writing competition. His goal is to write an entire mystery novel in a month. If he writes 5 chapters per week, how many chapters can he finish in 4 weeks?

_____ chapters

Joshua wants to buy a navy-blue raincoat for $30. If he pays with $5 bills, how many bills will he need?

_____ bills

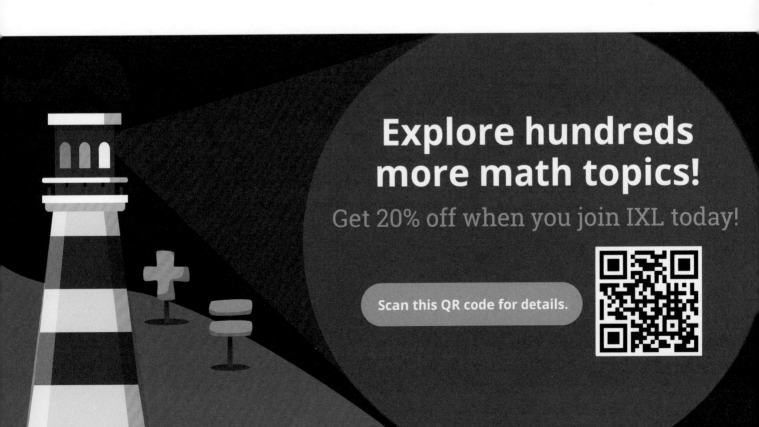

**Multiply. Draw a line to the correct answer.**

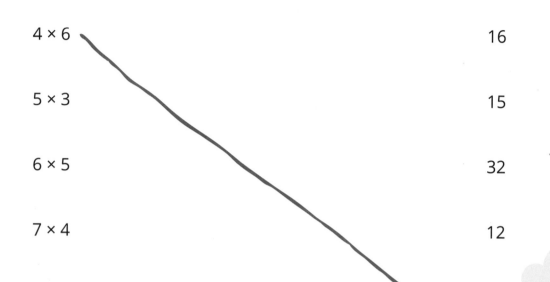

| | |
|---|---|
| 4 × 6 | 16 |
| 5 × 3 | 15 |
| 6 × 5 | 32 |
| 7 × 4 | 12 |
| 5 × 9 | 28 |
| 8 × 4 | 24 |
| 4 × 4 | 36 |
| 5 × 2 | 20 |
| 4 × 9 | 45 |
| 7 × 5 | 10 |
| 5 × 4 | 35 |
| 4 × 3 | 30 |

**Multiply.**

$2 \times 4 =$ _____

$5 \times 1 =$ _____

$3 \times 6 =$ _____

$7 \times 4 =$ _____

$5 \times 7 =$ _____

$2 \times 6 =$ _____

$8 \times 2 =$ _____

$3 \times 8 =$ _____

$4 \times 4 =$ _____

$9 \times 2 =$ _____

$3 \times 4 =$ _____

$5 \times 2 =$ _____

$5 \times 9 =$ _____

$3 \times 9 =$ _____

$10 \times 3 =$ _____

$4 \times 5 =$ _____

$1 \times 4 =$ _____

$3 \times 3 =$ _____

$5 \times 5 =$ _____

$7 \times 2 =$ _____

IXL.com
skill ID
**DW5**

**Answer each question.**

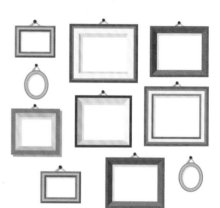

$2 each!

$6 each!

$10 each!

How much do 4 plants cost? _____

How many mugs can you buy for $18? _____ mugs

What costs more, 5 plants or 2 mugs? _____

How much would it cost to buy 2 plants, 2 mugs, and 2 picture frames? _____

You have 8 five-dollar bills. How many picture frames can you buy? _____ frames

**Write the missing numbers.**

_____ × 5 = 15          3 × _____ = 21          2 × _____ = 2

10 × 2 = _____          8 × _____ = 32          4 × 3 = _____

_____ × 6 = 24          _____ × 10 = 50          _____ × 4 = 40

5 × _____ = 30          3 × _____ = 6          2 × _____ = 4

_____ × 4 = 36          8 × _____ = 40          _____ × 5 = 20

2 × 9 = _____          4 × _____ = 16          _____ × 8 = 24

For more practice, visit IXL.com or the IXL mobile app and enter this code in the search bar.

IXL.com
skill ID
ZEY

Follow the path!

If you land on a product that is less than 12, go to the right one square.

If you land on a product that is equal to 12, go down one square.

If you land on a product that is more than 12, go to the left one square.

START ⬇

| | | | | | |
|---|---|---|---|---|---|
| 4 × 6 | 3 × 3 | 2 × 3 | 1 × 4 | 3 × 4 | 4 × 7 |
| 6 × 5 | 6 × 2 | 4 × 4 | 2 × 7 | 5 × 3 | 6 × 1 |
| 5 × 2 | 4 × 3 | 1 × 3 | 5 × 3 | 2 × 2 | 1 × 2 |
| 4 × 1 | 5 × 2 | 3 × 3 | 3 × 4 | 4 × 1 | 4 × 3 |
| 2 × 2 | 4 × 6 | 4 × 2 | 1 × 5 | 2 × 6 | 5 × 5 |

FINISH ⬇

IXL.com
skill ID
REN

**Answer each question.**

Marie is a dancer with the Richmond Ballet
Company. If Marie performs 5 times a week, how
many times will she perform in 6 weeks?

_____ times

A chocolate factory can make 4 chocolate bars
every second. How many chocolate bars can it
make in 8 seconds?

_____ bars

For a project, Mr. Garza divided his Spanish class
into 5 groups. Each group made an 8-minute movie.
How long will it take Mr. Garza to watch all of
the movies?

_____ minutes

Mason wants to buy 3 bags of kettle corn. Each bag
costs $6. If he has a $20 bill, does he have enough
money to buy all 3 bags?

_____

Tara bought 4 baskets of strawberries for $5 each. Lisa bought 3 baskets of
strawberries for $6 each. Who paid more, and by how much?

_____

Multiply. Compare the products in each pair. What do you notice?

3 × 7 = _____          4 × 6 = _____

7 × 3 = _____          6 × 4 = _____

5 × 8 = _____          3 × 9 = _____

8 × 5 = _____          9 × 3 = _____

4 × 8 = _____          5 × 6 = _____

8 × 4 = _____          6 × 5 = _____

**Multiply.**

$6 \times 1 =$ _____

$6 \times 2 =$ _____

$6 \times 3 =$ _____

$6 \times 4 =$ _____

$6 \times 5 =$ _____

$6 \times 6 =$ _____

$6 \times 7 =$ _____

$6 \times 8 =$ _____

$6 \times 9 =$ _____

$6 \times 10 =$ _____

**UNLOCK THE SECRET!** What do the multiples of 6 have in common? Are they also multiples of 2? Of 3? Of 4 or 5?

### Let's Learn!

All multiples of 6 are also multiples of 2 and 3. So, all multiples of 6 have these things in common:

- They are all even numbers.

- Their digits add up to a multiple of 3.

If both of these things are true, the number must be a multiple of 6!

**Try it yourself! Circle all the multiples of 6.**

| 90 | 146 | 513 | 1,152 |
|---|---|---|---|
| 14,580 | 530,192 | 10,450,236 | 3 million |

**Ready for an extra challenge? Write the missing digit to make each number a multiple of 6. There may be more than one correct answer.**

92___          3,7___4          57___,322

**Multiply.**

6 × 4 = _____

6 × 6 = _____

6 × 8 = _____

9 × 6 = _____

4 × 6 = _____

10 × 6 = _____

6 × 2 = _____

6 × 5 = _____

6 × 6 = _____

1 × 6 = _____

8 × 6 = _____

6 × 10 = _____

3 × 6 = _____

5 × 6 = _____

6 × 1 = _____

6 × 9 = _____

6 × 7 = _____

6 × 3 = _____

2 × 6 = _____

7 × 6 = _____

IXL.com
skill ID
**SX6**

How many days are there in a week? How about in 4 weeks? **Multiply by 7 to find the number of days for each number of weeks.**

| Number of weeks | Weeks × days per week | Total number of days |
|:---:|:---:|:---:|
| 1 | 1 × 7 | |
| 2 | 2 × 7 | |
| 3 | 3 × 7 | |
| 4 | 4 × 7 | |
| 5 | 5 × 7 | |
| 6 | 6 × 7 | |
| 7 | 7 × 7 | |
| 8 | 8 × 7 | |
| 9 | 9 × 7 | |
| 10 | 10 × 7 | |

**Multiply.**

7 × 5 = _____          7 × 8 = _____

3 × 7 = _____          7 × 1 = _____

7 × 4 = _____          6 × 7 = _____

7 × 9 = _____          5 × 7 = _____

4 × 7 = _____          7 × 10 = _____

10 × 7 = _____          7 × 7 = _____

7 × 2 = _____          9 × 7 = _____

8 × 7 = _____          7 × 3 = _____

7 × 6 = _____          1 × 7 = _____

2 × 7 = _____          7 × 7 = _____

IXL.com
skill ID
**9PT**

**Answer each question.**

If you run 3 miles every day for one whole week, how many miles have you run?

_____ miles

Ryan brought 2 six-packs of water bottles to his team's soccer game. How many bottles were there in all?

_____ bottles

Natasha sews dog socks in her spare time. If she makes 4 socks each for 7 dogs, how many socks is that in all?

_____ socks

If a box of donuts costs $7, how much would it cost to buy 8 boxes?

_____

Mr. Weber planted 4 rows of tulips with 7 tulips in each row. Mrs. Johnson planted 5 rows of tulips with 6 tulips in each row. Who planted more tulips?

_____

**Solve the logic puzzle.**

Allison, Zoe, Dave, Chris, and Sandra all live on the same block. Their ages are 6, 7, 12, 13, and 14, in some order. Use the clues to figure out how old everyone is!

Chris is twice as old as Sandra.

Zoe is twice as old as Allison.

Dave is younger than Chris.

| Age | Allison | Zoe | Dave | Chris | Sandra |
|-----|---------|-----|------|-------|--------|
| 6   |         |     |      |       |        |
| 7   |         |     |      |       |        |
| 12  |         |     |      |       |        |
| 13  |         |     |      |       |        |
| 14  |         |     |      |       |        |

**Solve each riddle.**

I'm a multiple of 7. I'm less than 40 and greater than 20. My digits add up to 8. What number am I?

If you multiply me by 4 and then subtract 4, you get a number that is 6 times 4. What number am I?

If you multiply me by 6, you get the same product as 3 times 4. What number am I?

**Let's Learn!**

Sometimes you need to multiply more than two numbers together. To do it, multiply two numbers together at a time. You can use parentheses to show which pair to do first.

$$2 \times 2 \times 3 = (2 \times 2) \times 3 = 4 \times 3 = 12$$

You can group the factors in any way. You'll get the same answer each time!

$$2 \times 2 \times 3 = 2 \times (2 \times 3) = 2 \times 6 = 12$$

**Try it yourself! Show how to multiply each group of factors in two different ways.**

$2 \times 3 \times 3$
$$(2 \times 3) \times 3 = \underline{6 \times 3} = \underline{18}$$
$$2 \times (3 \times 3) = \underline{2 \times 9} = \underline{18}$$

$3 \times 2 \times 5$
$$\underline{\hspace{3cm}} = \underline{\hspace{2cm}} = \underline{\hspace{1.5cm}}$$
$$\underline{\hspace{3cm}} = \underline{\hspace{2cm}} = \underline{\hspace{1.5cm}}$$

$2 \times 2 \times 4$
$$\underline{\hspace{3cm}} = \underline{\hspace{2cm}} = \underline{\hspace{1.5cm}}$$
$$\underline{\hspace{3cm}} = \underline{\hspace{2cm}} = \underline{\hspace{1.5cm}}$$

**Show how to multiply each group of factors in two different ways.**

$1 \times 3 \times 2 \times 4$
$\underline{(1 \times 3) \times 2 \times 4} = \underline{3 \times (2 \times 4)} = \underline{3 \times 8} = \underline{24}$

_____ = _____ = _____ = _____

$3 \times 2 \times 2 \times 1$
_____ = _____ = _____ = _____

_____ = _____ = _____ = _____

**KEEP GOING!** See if you can come up with even more ways to solve either of the multiplication problems above.

**Challenge yourself! Find the missing number.**

$2 \times 3 \times \underline{\phantom{xxxx}} = 12$       $3 \times 2 \times \underline{\phantom{xxxx}} = 18$       $3 \times 3 \times \underline{\phantom{xxxx}} = 27$

For more practice, visit IXL.com or the IXL mobile app and enter this code in the search bar.

IXL.com skill ID

**5EC**

Camila is making pies for a bake sale. She plans to cut each pie into 8 slices. **Multiply by 8 to help her find the total number of slices!**

| Number of pies | Pies × slices per pie | Total slices of pie |
|---|---|---|
| 1 | 1 × 8 | |
| 2 | 2 × 8 | |
| 3 | 3 × 8 | |
| 4 | 4 × 8 | |
| 5 | 5 × 8 | |
| 6 | 6 × 8 | |
| 7 | 7 × 8 | |
| 8 | 8 × 8 | |
| 9 | 9 × 8 | |
| 10 | 10 × 8 | |

**FIND THE PATTERN!** | Look at the last digits of the multiples of 8. Can you find the pattern? What will the last digit of 8 × 13 be?

**Multiply.**

8 × 5 = _____          8 × 8 = _____

3 × 8 = _____          8 × 1 = _____

8 × 4 = _____          2 × 8 = _____

8 × 9 = _____          5 × 8 = _____

4 × 8 = _____          8 × 10 = _____

10 × 8 = _____          8 × 7 = _____

8 × 2 = _____          9 × 8 = _____

8 × 8 = _____          8 × 3 = _____

6 × 8 = _____          1 × 8 = _____

7 × 8 = _____          8 × 6 = _____

IXL.com
skill ID
**SMR**

### Let's Learn!

Here's a quick way to tell whether a large number is a multiple of 8! A number is a multiple of 8 if the last three digits form a number that is a multiple of 8.

Try it for 12,016. Look at the last three digits. They make the number 016, which is the same as 16. The number 16 is a multiple of 8. So, 12,016 is also a multiple of 8.

12,016        016 = 16        16 = 8 × 2

**Try it yourself! Circle the multiples of 8.**

| | | |
|---|---|---|
| 1,040 | 3,053 | 5,072 |
| 12,044 | 336,024 | 1,009,008 |
| 15,349,012 | 948,302,048 | 2,491,394,035 |

Multiply.

9 × 1 = _____

9 × 2 = _____

9 × 3 = _____

9 × 4 = _____

9 × 5 = _____

9 × 6 = _____

9 × 7 = _____

9 × 8 = _____

9 × 9 = _____

9 × 10 = _____

**FIND THE PATTERN!** | What do the digits of each answer add up to?

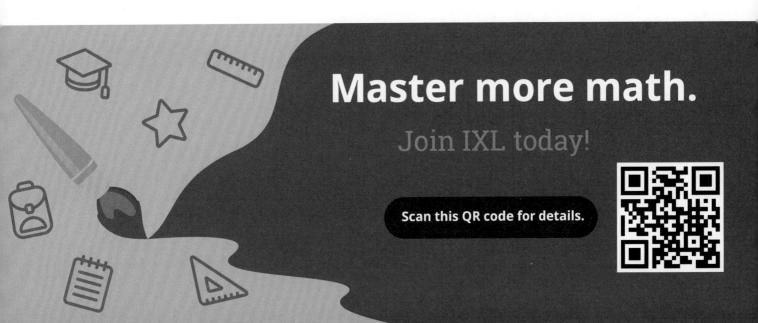

# Exploration Zone

## MULTIPLY BY 9 WITH YOUR FINGERS!

You can use your hands to multiply by 9! Start by holding your hands in front of you. Number each finger from 1 to 10, going from left to right.

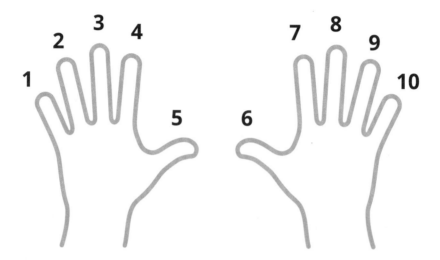

To multiply 9 by a number, lower that finger. For example, to multiply 9 × 8, lower your middle finger on your right hand.

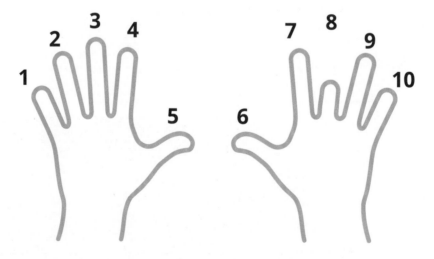

Now count the fingers to the left and to the right. The number of fingers to the left is the tens digit. The number of fingers to the right is the ones digit.

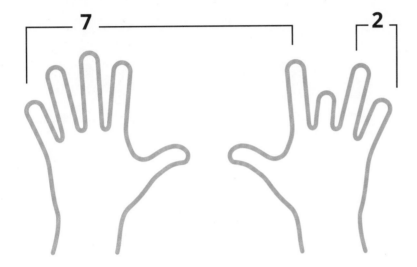

For 8 × 9, there are 7 fingers to the left and 2 fingers to the right.
That means that 9 × 8 is 72!

## TRY IT FOR YOURSELF!

## Can you solve 9 × 5 on your hands?

For an extra challenge, think about why this method works.

**Multiply.**

9 × 4 = _____

9 × 7 = _____

3 × 9 = _____

4 × 9 = _____

6 × 9 = _____

5 × 9 = _____

9 × 1 = _____

9 × 6 = _____

9 × 9 = _____

9 × 10 = _____

10 × 9 = _____

9 × 8 = _____

2 × 9 = _____

9 × 9 = _____

8 × 9 = _____

9 × 3 = _____

9 × 5 = _____

9 × 2 = _____

1 × 9 = _____

7 × 9 = _____

**Write the missing numbers.**

$8 \times \underline{\hspace{1cm}} = 40$

$8 \times \underline{\hspace{1cm}} = 16$

$\underline{\hspace{1cm}} \times 8 = 80$

$\underline{\hspace{1cm}} \times 6 = 54$

$9 \times \underline{\hspace{1cm}} = 9$

$\underline{\hspace{1cm}} \times 9 = 27$

$\underline{\hspace{1cm}} \times 4 = 32$

$\underline{\hspace{1cm}} \times 5 = 45$

$8 \times \underline{\hspace{1cm}} = 64$

$4 \times 9 = \underline{\hspace{1cm}}$

$9 \times \underline{\hspace{1cm}} = 18$

$8 \times 3 = \underline{\hspace{1cm}}$

$\underline{\hspace{1cm}} \times 7 = 63$

$\underline{\hspace{1cm}} \times 6 = 48$

$9 \times \underline{\hspace{1cm}} = 72$

**Answer each question.**

Lucas entered the library's summer reading contest. If he reads 8 books a month for 3 months, how many books will he read?

_____ books

Sandy's family wants to buy matching sunglasses. How much would it cost to buy 5 pairs of sunglasses that cost $9 each?

_____

The cabins at Woodside Summer Camp are actually big tree houses! If 3 tree houses can fit a total of 27 campers, how many campers can fit in each one? Each tree house is the same size.

_____ campers

Max baked a gigantic wedding cake for a competition. The cake had 8 layers and was over 4 feet tall! If Max needed 6 eggs for every layer, how many eggs did he need for the cake?

_____ eggs

Taylor is having a tea party for her friends, and she wants to have at least 5 mini muffins per person. If one recipe makes 36 mini muffins, and there will be 8 people, is one recipe enough?

_____

**Multiply.**

$7 \times 3 = $ _____

$6 \times 1 = $ _____

$4 \times 9 = $ _____

$4 \times 8 = $ _____

$5 \times 6 = $ _____

$7 \times 9 = $ _____

$6 \times 9 = $ _____

$6 \times 4 = $ _____

$8 \times 8 = $ _____

$5 \times 7 = $ _____

$3 \times 9 = $ _____

$10 \times 8 = $ _____

$7 \times 6 = $ _____

$6 \times 2 = $ _____

$2 \times 8 = $ _____

$7 \times 7 = $ _____

$1 \times 9 = $ _____

$8 \times 6 = $ _____

$7 \times 10 = $ _____

$4 \times 7 = $ _____

Pizza time! Answer each question.

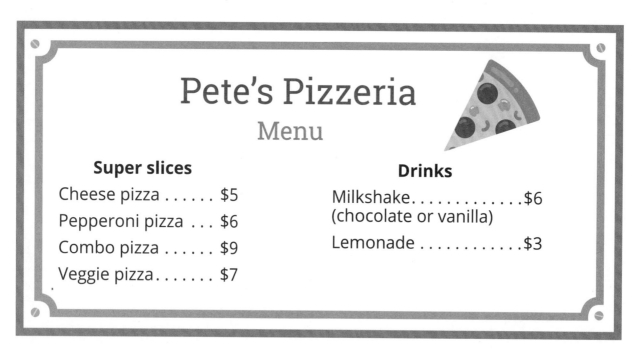

## Pete's Pizzeria
### Menu

**Super slices**

Cheese pizza . . . . . . $5

Pepperoni pizza . . . $6

Combo pizza . . . . . . $9

Veggie pizza . . . . . . . $7

**Drinks**

Milkshake. . . . . . . . . . . . $6
(chocolate or vanilla)

Lemonade . . . . . . . . . . . $3

How much would 3 slices of veggie pizza cost?  _____

What costs more, 4 slices of combo pizza or 6 slices of cheese pizza?  _____

Dylan's family bought 3 slices of cheese pizza, 3 slices of pepperoni pizza, and 4 milkshakes. How much did their meal cost?  _____

IXL.com
skill ID
**9TA**

How much more would 4 slices of veggie pizza cost than 4 slices of pepperoni pizza?

_____

**Answer each question.**

The Milltown Orchestra gives 3 concerts every month. How many concerts will they give in 8 months?

_____ concerts

In a math contest, each question is worth 6 points. If a team answers 7 questions correctly, how many points will they have?

_____ points

Jasmine is painting 3 of the rooms in her house. She bought 7 cans of paint, and each can has 4 quarts of paint in it. If it takes 8 quarts to paint each room, does Jasmine have enough paint for all 3 rooms?

_____

Carlos wants to buy 5 posters that cost $9 each. He has 2 twenty-dollar bills. How much more money does he need?

_____

IXL.com
skill ID
Z46

Multiply. Draw a line between the matching answers.

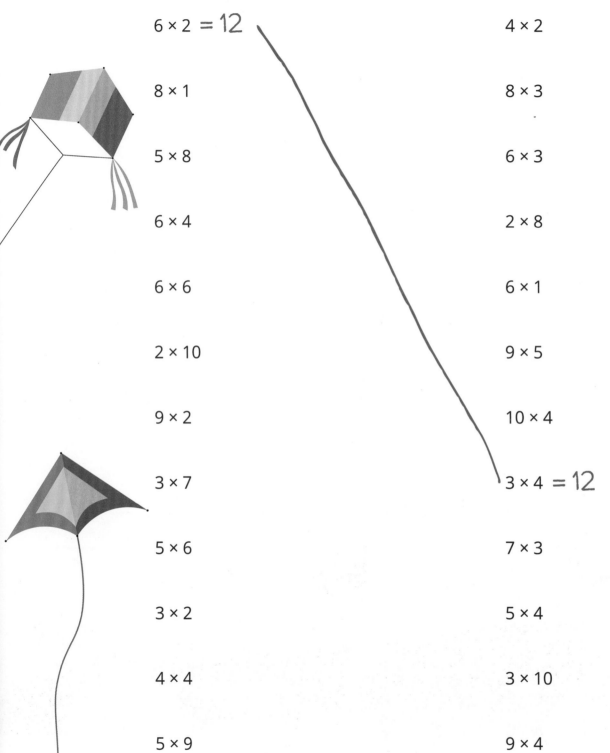

6 × 2 = 12                                   4 × 2

8 × 1                                        8 × 3

5 × 8                                        6 × 3

6 × 4                                        2 × 8

6 × 6                                        6 × 1

2 × 10                                       9 × 5

9 × 2                                        10 × 4

3 × 7                                        3 × 4 = 12

5 × 6                                        7 × 3

3 × 2                                        5 × 4

4 × 4                                        3 × 10

5 × 9                                        9 × 4

A decade is 10 years. How many years are there in 2 decades? How about in 3 decades? **Multiply by 10 to find out!**

| Number of decades | Decades × number of years in a decade | Total number of years |
|:---:|:---:|:---:|
| 1 | 1 × 10 | |
| 2 | 2 × 10 | |
| 3 | 3 × 10 | |
| 4 | 4 × 10 | |
| 5 | 5 × 10 | |
| 6 | 6 × 10 | |
| 7 | 7 × 10 | |
| 8 | 8 × 10 | |
| 9 | 9 × 10 | |
| 10 | 10 × 10 | |

**KEEP IT GOING!** What pattern do you see? What do you think 11 × 10 will be? How about 23 × 10?

**Multiply.**

10 × 3 = _____          10 × 2 = _____

6 × 10 = _____          1 × 10 = _____

10 × 8 = _____          5 × 10 = _____

2 × 10 = _____          10 × 4 = _____

9 × 10 = _____          10 × 5 = _____

3 × 10 = _____          10 × 7 = _____

10 × 1 = _____          10 × 6 = _____

7 × 10 = _____          10 × 10 = _____

10 × 10 = _____          10 × 9 = _____

4 × 10 = _____          8 × 10 = _____

IXL.com
skill ID
**6YD**

---

**Let's Learn!**

As you saw on page 53, all multiples of 10 end in 0. If you see a number that ends in 0, it must be a multiple of 10!

---

**Try it yourself! Circle the multiples of 10.**

| | | | | |
|---|---|---|---|---|
| 160 | 204 | 425 | 60 | 700 |
| 1,003 | 40,030 | 524,102 | 1 million | 1 trillion |

---

**Answer each question.**

Ravenswood Sports Camp bought 7 tennis rackets for $10 each. How much did the tennis rackets cost in all?

_____

A rollercoaster can fit 10 people in each car. How many cars do you need for 40 people?

_____ cars

Ruby has 6 dimes. How much money is that?

_____ cents

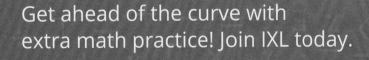

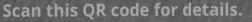

## MULTIPLYING BY MULTIPLES OF 10

You know 4 × 6, but how about 4 × 60? How about 4 × 600? Think about another way to write those problems.

4 × 60 = 4 × 6 tens

4 × 60 = 24 tens

4 × 60 = 240

4 × 600 = 4 × 6 hundreds

4 × 600 = 24 hundreds

4 × 600 = 2,400

Can you find the pattern?

4 × 60 = 240

4 × 600 = 2,400

4 × 6,000 = _____

4 × 60,000 = _____

4 × 600,000 = _____

IXL.com
skill ID
**DC9**

**TRY IT YOURSELF!**

Multiply.

5 × 3,000 = _____

2 × 90,000 = _____

9 × 60,000 = _____

7 × 400,000 = _____

6 × 700,000 = _____

8 × 5,000,000 = _____

# PROBLEMS WITH MULTIPLES OF 10

You can use patterns with multiples of 10 to solve problems with big numbers. For example, if an olive oil factory fills 500 bottles in a day, how many bottles will it fill in 3 days?

$$3 \times 500 = 1,500$$

The factory will fill 1,500 bottles in 3 days!

IXL.com
skill ID
**83B**

## TRY IT YOURSELF!

Answer each question.

It costs $3 to ride the train. If Amy rides the train twice every day for 100 days, how much will she need to pay?

_____

A swimming pool has 20,000 gallons of water. How much water would there be in 5 swimming pools?

_____ gallons

A baseball team sells about 3,000,000 tickets each season. How many tickets does it sell in 3 seasons?

_____ tickets

**Multiply.**

3 × 6 = _____

9 × 2 = _____

4 × 4 = _____

6 × 5 = _____

10 × 5 = _____

7 × 3 = _____

4 × 9 = _____

3 × 4 = _____

2 × 8 = _____

6 × 6 = _____

4 × 8 = _____

6 × 4 = _____

7 × 9 = _____

2 × 10 = _____

7 × 7 = _____

5 × 5 = _____

9 × 6 = _____

5 × 8 = _____

7 × 6 = _____

8 × 7 = _____

Find the path from A to B. You may step only on stones that are more than 25 but less than 45.

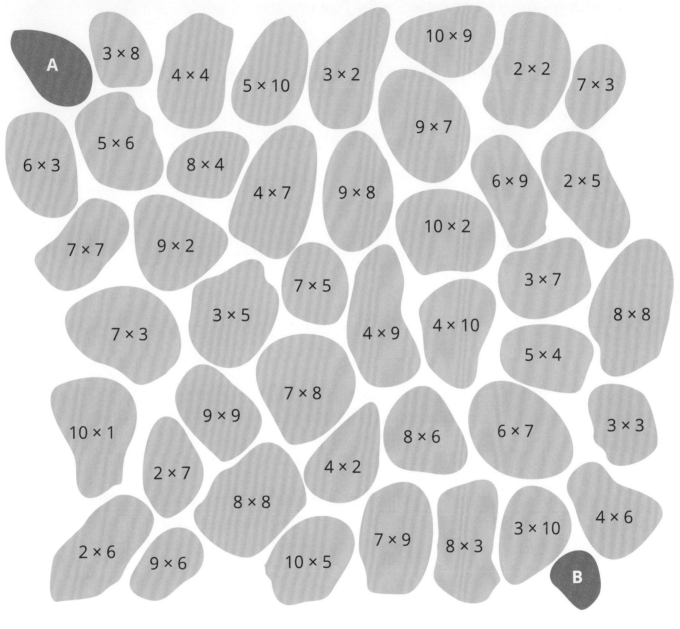

**Solve each riddle.**

If you multiply me by 4, you get 5 × 8. What am I?

I am a multiple of 7. I am less than 4 × 10 and greater than 5 × 6. What am I?

If you multiply me by 6, you get 5 × 10 minus 2. What am I?

---

**Solve each problem.**

Use the numbers 2, 3, 4, and 6 to write two multiplication sentences with the same product.

Write at least two multiplication sentences that have a product of 24. *For an extra challenge, see if you can come up with more!*

Write a multiplication sentence with factors 5 and 8. Then write another multiplication sentence with different factors but the same product.

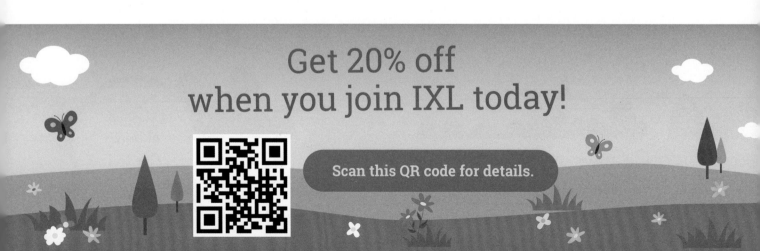

**Write the missing numbers.**

3 × _____ = 24          _____ × 2 = 14          9 × 9 = _____

_____ × 8 = 48          2 × _____ = 18          10 × _____ = 70

5 × 4 = _____           9 × _____ = 45          3 × _____ = 15

_____ × 7 = 35          9 × 4 = _____           8 × _____ = 64

3 × _____ = 27          9 × 8 = _____           _____ × 3 = 24

_____ × 6 = 60          7 × _____ = 49          6 × 9 = _____

IXL.com
skill ID
**FZA**

## Let's Learn!

If you know 4 × 10 and 4 × 3, then you can multiply 4 × 13, too! Look at the model below to see how.

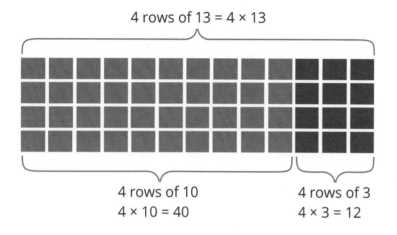

4 rows of 13 = 4 × 13

4 rows of 10
4 × 10 = 40

4 rows of 3
4 × 3 = 12

As you can see, you can split 4 × 13 into two easier problems.

4 × 13 = 4 × (10 + 3)

4 × 13 = (4 × 10) + (4 × 3)

4 × 13 = 40 + 12

4 × 13 = 52

**Fill in the blanks.**

To help, pick numbers that are easy to multiply, like 10.

5 × 16 = 5 × ( __10__ + __6__ )

5 × 16 = ( 5 × __10__ ) + ( 5 × __6__ )

5 × 16 = __50__ + __30__

5 × 16 = __80__

**Fill in the blanks.**

7 × 15 = 7 × ( _____ + _____ )

7 × 15 = ( 7 × _____ ) + ( 7 × _____ )

7 × 15 = _____ + _____

7 × 15 = _____


4 × 18 = 4 × ( _____ + _____ )

4 × 18 = ( 4 × _____ ) + ( 4 × _____ )

4 × 18 = _____ + _____

4 × 18 = _____


8 × 19 = 8 × ( _____ + _____ )

8 × 19 = ( 8 × _____ ) + ( 8 × _____ )

8 × 19 = _____ + _____

8 × 19 = _____

For more practice, visit IXL.com or the IXL mobile app and enter this code in the search bar.

IXL.com
skill ID
**QXM**

**Multiply.**

If you multiply any number by 0, the answer is always 0.

$0 \times 1 = \underline{\phantom{0}0\phantom{0}}$

$0 \times 6 = \underline{\phantom{0000}}$

$0 \times 2 = \underline{\phantom{0000}}$

$0 \times 7 = \underline{\phantom{0000}}$

$0 \times 3 = \underline{\phantom{0000}}$

$0 \times 8 = \underline{\phantom{0000}}$

$0 \times 4 = \underline{\phantom{0000}}$

$0 \times 9 = \underline{\phantom{0000}}$

$0 \times 5 = \underline{\phantom{0000}}$

$0 \times 10 = \underline{\phantom{0000}}$

**KEEP IT GOING!** | Can you solve $0 \times 25$? How about $0 \times 4{,}000{,}000$?

IXL.com
skill ID
**BGK**

## Multiply.

If you multiply any number by 1, the answer is always that number.

1 × 7 = ___7___         3 × 1 = _____

2 × 1 = _____          1 × 5 = _____

10 × 1 = _____         7 × 1 = _____

1 × 8 = _____          1 × 1 = _____

6 × 1 = _____          4 × 1 = _____

1 × 2 = _____          5 × 1 = _____

1 × 9 = _____          1 × 6 = _____

## Challenge yourself! Multiply.

1 × 48 = _____

327 × 1 = _____

33,250 × 1 = _____

1 × 5,034,150 = _____

**Multiply.**

11 × 1 = _____             11 × 6 = _____

11 × 2 = _____             11 × 7 = _____

11 × 3 = _____             11 × 8 = _____

11 × 4 = _____             11 × 9 = _____

11 × 5 = _____             11 × 10 = _____

**UNLOCK THE SECRET!** | Can you find the pattern in the first nine products above?

IXL.com
skill ID
**AZJ**

A **dozen** is 12 of something. So, if you buy a dozen donuts, you are buying 12 donuts. **Multiply by 12 to find the total number of donuts!**

| Dozens of donuts | Dozens × number of donuts in one dozen | Total number of donuts |
|---|---|---|
| 1 | $1 \times 12$ | |
| 2 | $2 \times 12$ | |
| 3 | $3 \times 12$ | |
| 4 | $4 \times 12$ | |
| 5 | $5 \times 12$ | |
| 6 | $6 \times 12$ | |
| 7 | $7 \times 12$ | |
| 8 | $8 \times 12$ | |
| 9 | $9 \times 12$ | |
| 10 | $10 \times 12$ | |
| 11 | $11 \times 12$ | |
| 12 | $12 \times 12$ | |

**DIG DEEPER!** Look at the multiples of 12. What other numbers are they multiples of? How can you tell?

IXL.com
skill ID
**8NV**

**Answer each question.**

At Dickinson Drama Camp, the campers are split into 4 groups of 11. How many campers are there in all?

_____ campers

Robbie's youngest sister is 3 feet tall. How many inches is that? Remember, there are 12 inches in a foot.

_____ inches

Maria's favorite cookie recipe makes 2 dozen cookies in each batch. If she makes 2 batches, how many cookies will she have in all?

_____ cookies

Brady gives surfing lessons every Saturday. Each class lasts for 2 hours, and there are 11 people in each class. How many people can Brady teach in 6 hours?

_____ people

**Multiply. Draw a line to the correct answer.**

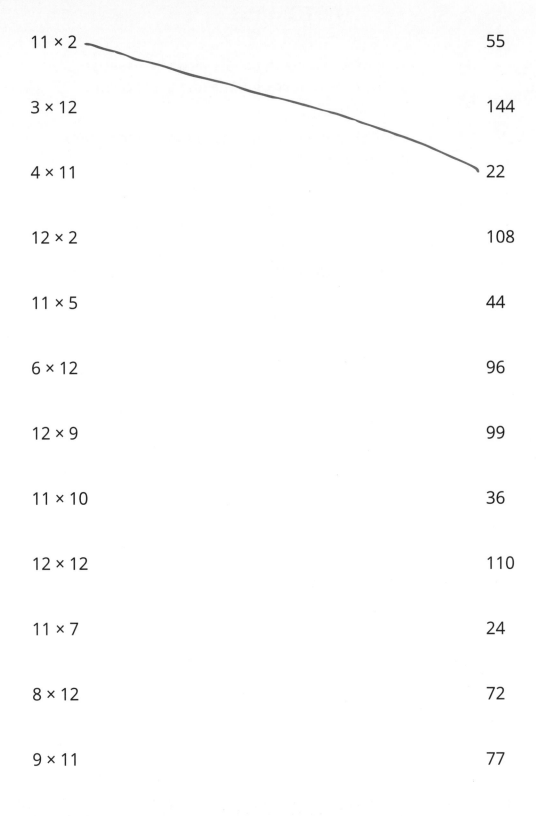

| | |
|---|---|
| 11 × 2 | 55 |
| 3 × 12 | 144 |
| 4 × 11 | 22 |
| 12 × 2 | 108 |
| 11 × 5 | 44 |
| 6 × 12 | 96 |
| 12 × 9 | 99 |
| 11 × 10 | 36 |
| 12 × 12 | 110 |
| 11 × 7 | 24 |
| 8 × 12 | 72 |
| 9 × 11 | 77 |

## FACTORIALS

**5!**

The number 5 is great, but 5! is actually a special number called a **factorial**. The number 5! is read "five factorial."

To find 5!, multiply the number 5 by all of the whole numbers below it.

$$5! = 5 \times 4 \times 3 \times 2 \times 1 = 120$$

### TRY IT YOURSELF!

### Solve.

2! = _____          3! = _____

4! = _____

### Grab a calculator and keep going!

7! = _____          10! = _____

12! = _____

**Multiply.**

3 × 11 = _____          4 × 6 = _____

8 × 8 = _____          12 × 5 = _____

10 × 7 = _____          6 × 9 = _____

6 × 11 = _____          0 × 5 = _____

7 × 8 = _____          3 × 7 = _____

8 × 12 = _____          9 × 1 = _____

5 × 5 = _____          11 × 0 = _____

4 × 8 = _____          12 × 4 = _____

1 × 7 = _____          11 × 12 = _____

5 × 10 = _____          9 × 12 = _____

**Write the missing numbers.**

6 × _____ = 36

_____ × 2 = 22

9 × 7 = _____

_____ × 8 = 96

3 × _____ = 18

12 × _____ = 60

3 × 11 = _____

9 × _____ = 54

7 × _____ = 56

_____ × 5 = 40

12 × 4 = _____

8 × _____ = 88

9 × _____ = 27

6 × 7 = _____

_____ × 12 = 84

IXL.com
skill ID
**WB8**

**Answer each question.**

Emmylou bought 7 packs of hot dogs for her class camping trip. There are 8 hot dogs in each pack. How many hot dogs did Emmylou buy?

_____ hot dogs

Steve has 4 vases, and he puts a dozen roses in each. How many roses does Steve put in the vases?

_____ roses

Maverick has 4 boxes with 6 wind-up cars in each box. If Maverick shares the wind-up cars equally with his sister, how many cars will each of them get?

_____ cars

A pet store has 55 fish. If each fish bowl holds 5 fish, how many fish bowls does the store need?

_____ fish bowls

IXL.com
skill ID
F6C

## PERFECT SQUARES

What do the numbers 4, 9, and 16 have in common?
To figure it out, write a multiplication sentence for each model.

$\underline{2} \times \underline{2} = \underline{4}$        ___ × ___ = ___        ___ × ___ = ___

The numbers 4, 9, and 16 are all special numbers. They are called
**perfect squares**. A perfect square is the product of a number times itself.

**TRY IT YOURSELF!**

IXL.com
skill ID
**GMM**

### Find the perfect squares.

5 × 5 = _____        1 × 1 = _____

6 × 6 = _____        7 × 7 = _____

8 × 8 = _____        9 × 9 = _____

### Circle the perfect squares.

| 9 | 30 | 25 | 49 | 55 |
|---|----|----|----|----|
| 16 | 46 | 70 | 36 | 100 |

# ADDING UP THE ODDS

Check it out! All perfect squares are equal to the sum of a series of odd numbers. Do you see the pattern below?

$$1 = 1$$
$$4 = 1 + 3$$
$$9 = 1 + 3 + 5$$
$$16 = 1 + 3 + 5 + 7$$
$$25 = 1 + 3 + 5 + 7 + 9$$

Look at the square models below. **Circle the squares that are added to the previous square number. Then count how many squares you have circled. The first two have been done for you. What do you notice?**

   1        3        \_\_\_       \_\_\_

\_\_\_        \_\_\_

**Let's Learn!**

What if you want to multiply bigger numbers, like 62 × 4? Just follow these steps!

First, multiply the ones.

```
  6 2
×   4
─────
    8
```

2 ones × 4 = 8 ones

Then, multiply the tens.

```
  6 2
×   4
─────
2 4 8
```

6 tens × 4 = 24 tens
24 tens = 2 hundreds and 4 tens

So, 62 × 4 is 248!

**Try it yourself! Multiply.**

```
  1 4          2 3          3 4
×   2        ×   2        ×   2
```

```
  7 3          6 2          6 1
×   3        ×   3        ×   5
```

**Multiply.**

$$\begin{array}{r} 5\,4 \\ \times\ \ 2 \\ \hline \end{array}$$

$$\begin{array}{r} 4\,2 \\ \times\ \ 3 \\ \hline \end{array}$$

$$\begin{array}{r} 6\,1 \\ \times\ \ 4 \\ \hline \end{array}$$

$$\begin{array}{r} 8\,3 \\ \times\ \ 3 \\ \hline \end{array}$$

$$\begin{array}{r} 8\,1 \\ \times\ \ 5 \\ \hline \end{array}$$

$$\begin{array}{r} 9\,3 \\ \times\ \ 2 \\ \hline \end{array}$$

$$\begin{array}{r} 8\,4 \\ \times\ \ 2 \\ \hline \end{array}$$

$$\begin{array}{r} 9\,2 \\ \times\ \ 4 \\ \hline \end{array}$$

$$\begin{array}{r} 7\,1 \\ \times\ \ 5 \\ \hline \end{array}$$

Boost your math learning and save 20%!

Scan this QR code or visit www.ixl.com/workbook/3m for details.

## Let's Learn!

Sometimes, you will need to regroup when you multiply. Look at 53 × 7 as an example.

First, multiply the ones.

$$\begin{array}{r} {}^{2}\phantom{0} \\ 5\,3 \\ \times\ \ 7 \\ \hline 1 \end{array}$$

3 ones × 7 = 21 ones

21 ones = 2 tens and 1 one

Write the ones below. Write the tens above to save them for later.

Next, multiply the **tens**.

$$\begin{array}{r} {}^{2}\phantom{0} \\ 5\,3 \\ \times\ \ 7 \\ \hline 3\,7\,1 \end{array}$$

5 tens × 7 = 35 tens

Now add in the extra tens you saved at the top.

35 tens + 2 tens = 37 tens

37 tens = 3 hundreds and 7 tens

Now read what you have left. The answer to 53 × 7 is 371!

**Try it yourself! Multiply.**

$$\begin{array}{r} 2\,4 \\ \times\ \ 6 \\ \hline \end{array} \qquad \begin{array}{r} 3\,3 \\ \times\ \ 5 \\ \hline \end{array} \qquad \begin{array}{r} 2\,6 \\ \times\ \ 3 \\ \hline \end{array}$$

$$\begin{array}{r} 3\,9 \\ \times\ \ 4 \\ \hline \end{array} \qquad \begin{array}{r} 4\,8 \\ \times\ \ 7 \\ \hline \end{array} \qquad \begin{array}{r} 7\,2 \\ \times\ \ 5 \\ \hline \end{array}$$

**Multiply.**

```
   4 3              5 5              4 6
 ×   4            ×   2            ×   3
```

```
   5 4              7 7              6 9
 ×   7            ×   8            ×   5
```

```
   6 7              3 8              7 5
 ×   3            ×   9            ×   6
```

```
   9 4              8 6              7 9
 ×   8            ×   9            ×   7
```

IXL.com
skill ID
9PM

**Answer each question.**

At her bake sale, Adalyn sold 22 brownies for $4 each. How much money did she make?

_____

There are 24 hours in a day. How many hours are there in 3 days?

_____ hours

At Rosemary Elementary School, there are 5 fourth-grade classes. Each class has 26 students. How many fourth-grade students are there at Rosemary Elementary?

_____ students

There are 9 people in the art club at Evelyn's school. This year, each person in the club painted 27 paintings for the art show. How many paintings did the art club make in total?

_____ paintings

Rudy's Restaurant has 34 tables. If each table seats 4 people, how many people can fit in Rudy's Restaurant?

_____ people

IXL.com
skill ID
X5D

## Let's Learn!

Want to multiply even bigger numbers, like 523 × 3? You can use the same steps!

Multiply the ones first.

$$
\begin{array}{r}
5\,2\,3 \\
\times \quad 3 \\
\hline
9
\end{array}
$$

3 ones × 3 = 9 ones

Next, multiply the tens.

$$
\begin{array}{r}
5\,2\,3 \\
\times \quad 3 \\
\hline
6\,9
\end{array}
$$

2 tens × 3 = 6 tens

Finally, multiply the hundreds.

$$
\begin{array}{r}
5\,2\,3 \\
\times \quad 3 \\
\hline
1,5\,6\,9
\end{array}
$$

5 hundreds × 3 = 15 hundreds

15 hundreds = 1 thousand and 5 hundreds

So, 523 × 3 = 1,569!

**Multiply.**

$$
\begin{array}{r}
1\,4\,4 \\
\times \quad 2 \\
\hline
\end{array}
\qquad
\begin{array}{r}
2\,3\,2 \\
\times \quad 3 \\
\hline
\end{array}
\qquad
\begin{array}{r}
3\,1\,3 \\
\times \quad 3 \\
\hline
\end{array}
$$

$$
\begin{array}{r}
3\,3\,4 \\
\times \quad 2 \\
\hline
\end{array}
\qquad
\begin{array}{r}
4\,2\,1 \\
\times \quad 4 \\
\hline
\end{array}
\qquad
\begin{array}{r}
5\,0\,1 \\
\times \quad 5 \\
\hline
\end{array}
$$

### Let's Learn!

Sometimes, you will need to regroup when you multiply bigger numbers. Here's how to multiply 564 × 3.

Multiply the ones first.

$$
\begin{array}{r}
{}^{2}\phantom{0} \\
5\,6\,4 \\
\times \quad 6 \\
\hline
4
\end{array}
$$

4 ones × 6 = 24 ones

Remember to regroup 24 ones into 2 tens and 4 ones.

Next, multiply the tens.

$$
\begin{array}{r}
{}^{3}\,{}^{2}\phantom{0} \\
5\,6\,4 \\
\times \quad 6 \\
\hline
8\,4
\end{array}
$$

6 tens × 6 = 36 tens

Remember to add 2 more to get 38 tens.

Regroup 38 tens into 3 hundreds and 8 tens.

Finally, multiply the hundreds.

$$
\begin{array}{r}
{}^{3}\,{}^{2}\phantom{0} \\
5\,6\,4 \\
\times \quad 6 \\
\hline
3,3\,8\,4
\end{array}
$$

5 hundreds × 6 = 30 hundreds

Remember to add 3 more to get 33 hundreds.

So, 564 × 6 = 3,384!

**Multiply.**

$$
\begin{array}{r}
2\,2\,4 \\
\times \quad 3 \\
\hline
\end{array}
\qquad
\begin{array}{r}
2\,4\,6 \\
\times \quad 4 \\
\hline
\end{array}
\qquad
\begin{array}{r}
5\,1\,8 \\
\times \quad 3 \\
\hline
\end{array}
$$

**Multiply.**

$$\begin{array}{r} 469 \\ \times \quad 5 \\ \hline \end{array}$$

$$\begin{array}{r} 522 \\ \times \quad 4 \\ \hline \end{array}$$

$$\begin{array}{r} 935 \\ \times \quad 8 \\ \hline \end{array}$$

$$\begin{array}{r} 443 \\ \times \quad 2 \\ \hline \end{array}$$

$$\begin{array}{r} 546 \\ \times \quad 7 \\ \hline \end{array}$$

$$\begin{array}{r} 283 \\ \times \quad 2 \\ \hline \end{array}$$

$$\begin{array}{r} 475 \\ \times \quad 5 \\ \hline \end{array}$$

$$\begin{array}{r} 956 \\ \times \quad 6 \\ \hline \end{array}$$

$$\begin{array}{r} 837 \\ \times \quad 7 \\ \hline \end{array}$$

$$\begin{array}{r} 679 \\ \times \quad 7 \\ \hline \end{array}$$

$$\begin{array}{r} 794 \\ \times \quad 8 \\ \hline \end{array}$$

$$\begin{array}{r} 795 \\ \times \quad 9 \\ \hline \end{array}$$

For more practice, visit IXL.com or the IXL mobile app and enter this code in the search bar.

IXL.com
skill ID
FA7

**Answer each question.**

Trevor bought 2 airplane tickets to Denver. If each ticket cost $342, how much did he pay?

_____

For their grand opening party, Avery's Cupcake Shop made vanilla, chocolate, and red velvet cupcakes. They made 144 cupcakes of each flavor. How many cupcakes did they make?

_____ cupcakes

Nate works at his aunt's smoothie shop. He earns $425 every month. How much does he earn in 4 months?

_____

Lila wants to organize her collection of 550 baseball cards into binders. If each binder can fit up to 114 cards, will 5 binders be enough?

_____

An ice cream factory has been making chocolate ice cream for the past 9 days. It made 852 cartons each day. How many cartons of chocolate ice cream did the factory make in all?

_____ cartons

IXL.com
skill ID
9GD

Multiply.

$$\begin{array}{r} 34 \\ \times\ 2 \\ \hline \end{array}$$

$$\begin{array}{r} 63 \\ \times\ 3 \\ \hline \end{array}$$

$$\begin{array}{r} 92 \\ \times\ 4 \\ \hline \end{array}$$

$$\begin{array}{r} 46 \\ \times\ 3 \\ \hline \end{array}$$

$$\begin{array}{r} 55 \\ \times\ 5 \\ \hline \end{array}$$

$$\begin{array}{r} 86 \\ \times\ 7 \\ \hline \end{array}$$

$$\begin{array}{r} 523 \\ \times\ \ 3 \\ \hline \end{array}$$

$$\begin{array}{r} 464 \\ \times\ \ 4 \\ \hline \end{array}$$

$$\begin{array}{r} 357 \\ \times\ \ 5 \\ \hline \end{array}$$

$$\begin{array}{r} 643 \\ \times\ \ 7 \\ \hline \end{array}$$

$$\begin{array}{r} 569 \\ \times\ \ 7 \\ \hline \end{array}$$

$$\begin{array}{r} 857 \\ \times\ \ 9 \\ \hline \end{array}$$

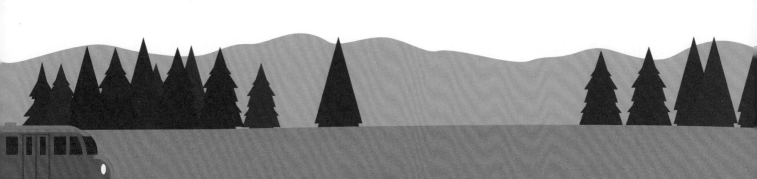

Use the recipe to answer each question.

## Casey's Chocolate Chip Cookies

195 grams flour

1 tsp. baking soda

½ tsp. salt

120 grams butter

105 grams brown sugar

95 grams granulated sugar

1 large egg

1 tsp. vanilla extract

450 grams chocolate chips

Preheat the oven to 350°F.

In a bowl, mix together the flour, baking soda, and salt.

In a separate bowl, blend together the butter and sugar. Then add the eggs and vanilla. Slowly add the flour mixture. Stir in the chocolate chips.

Scoop heaping tablespoons of dough onto a baking sheet. The balls of dough should be 2 inches apart. Bake for 11 to 13 minutes.

If you make 2 batches of Casey's Chocolate Chip Cookies, how much granulated sugar will you need?

_____ grams

If you make 3 batches of the cookies, how much flour will you need?

_____ grams

If you have 220 grams of brown sugar, do you have enough for 2 batches of cookies?

_____

If there are 3 dozen cookies in a batch, how many cookies does 2 batches make?

_____ cookies

**Answer each question.**

Kylie owns a skateboard shop. Yesterday, she sold 18 pairs of kneepads. Each pair of kneepads was $9. How much money did Kylie make from selling kneepads yesterday?

_____

For the past 3 days, Kylie has sold 18 pairs of kneepads every day. How many pairs of kneepads is that in all?

_____ pairs

How much money has Kylie made from selling kneepads over the past 3 days?

_____

If Kylie sells 126 pairs of kneepads in a week, how much money does she make?

_____

**Let's Learn!**

You have a rug that is 3 feet long and 5 feet wide. What is its **area**? You can use multiplication to find out!

To find the area of a shape, break the shape into unit squares. Count or multiply to find the area.

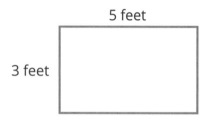

5 feet

3 feet

1 foot  1 foot  1 foot  1 foot  1 foot

1 foot

1 foot

1 foot

3 rows of 5 unit squares = 3 × 5 = 15 unit squares

In this problem, each unit square has an area of 1 square foot. So, the area of the rug is 15 square feet.

**Split each shape into unit squares. Write a multiplication sentence to find the area.**

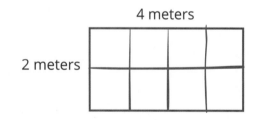

4 meters

2 meters

__2__ × __4__ = __8__ square meters

3 inches

3 inches

_____ × _____ = _____ square inches

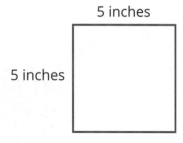

5 inches

5 inches

_____ × _____ = _____ square inches

6 meters

2 meters

_____ × _____ = _____ square meters

**Find the area of each shape.**

5 inches

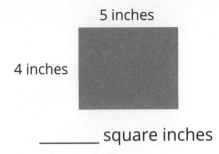

4 inches

_____ square inches

7 meters

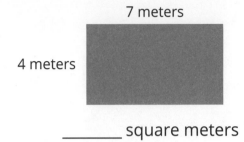

4 meters

_____ square meters

5 feet

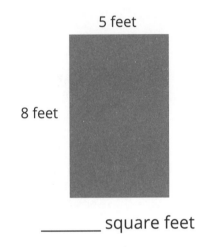

8 feet

_____ square feet

4 feet

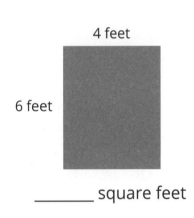

6 feet

_____ square feet

7 yards

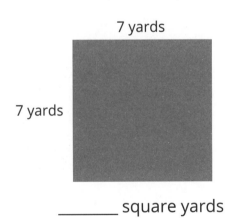

7 yards

_____ square yards

9 feet

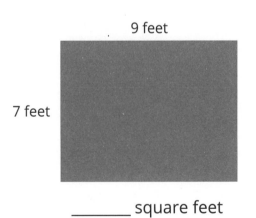

7 feet

_____ square feet

Write the missing side length.

### 6 INCHES

5 inches

Area = 30 square inches

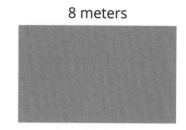

8 meters

Area = 40 square meters

4 yards

Area = 28 square yards

3 feet

Area = 21 square feet

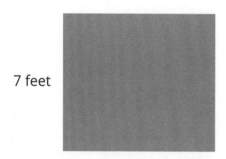

7 feet

Area = 56 square feet

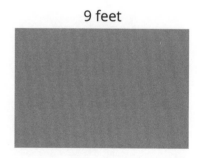

9 feet

Area = 54 square feet

**Answer each question.**

Cheyenne has a map of the world on her wall. It is 4 feet wide and 3 feet tall. What is its area?

_____ square feet

Angie wants to put a photograph on her wall. If the photograph is 8 inches by 10 inches, how much space will it take up?

_____ square inches

Grayson's favorite notebook is 6 inches tall and 4 inches wide. Amanda's favorite notebook is 8 inches tall and 5 inches wide. Whose notebook has a bigger area? By how much?

_____

A movie theater wants to save paper, so they decide to print smaller tickets. The old tickets were 3 inches by 7 inches. The new tickets are 2 inches by 6 inches. How much smaller are the new tickets?

_____

**Let's Learn!**

Can you find the area of this shape?

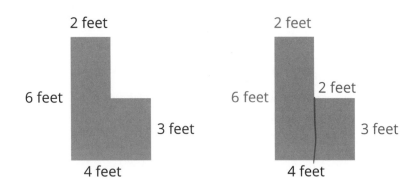

First, split it into two rectangles.

Then, subtract to find the missing side length.

Next, multiply to find the area of each rectangle, and then add to find the total area.

6 × 2 = 12 square feet          12 + 6 = 18 square feet

2 × 3 = 6 square feet

**Find the area of each shape.**

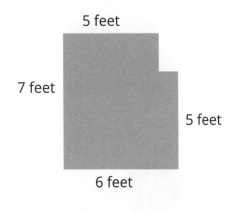

_____ square feet

_____ square yards

**Find the area of each shape.**

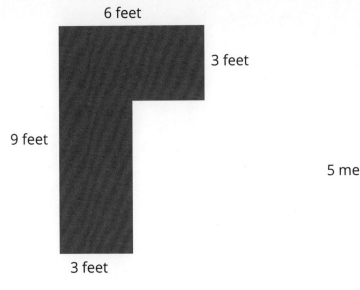

6 feet

3 feet

9 feet

3 feet

_____ square feet

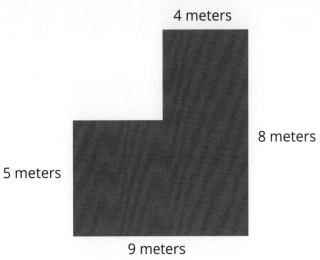

4 meters

8 meters

5 meters

9 meters

_____ square meters

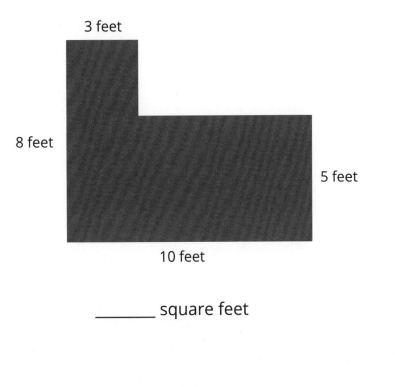

3 feet

8 feet

5 feet

10 feet

_____ square feet

**Show what you know! Multiply.**

3 × 6 = _____        4 × 5 = _____        1 × 12 = _____

8 × 5 = _____        0 × 8 = _____        11 × 6 = _____

7 × 4 = _____        3 × 9 = _____        6 × 9 = _____

10 × 7 = _____        12 × 4 = _____        8 × 7 = _____

---

**Write the missing numbers.**

_____ × 4 = 16        _____ × 9 = 9        8 × _____ = 48

3 × _____ = 24        7 × _____ = 35        0 × 5 = _____

_____ × 6 = 42        4 × 9 = _____        5 × _____ = 25

_____ × 11 = 99        12 × _____ = 60        _____ × 9 = 63

**Fill in the blanks. Multiply the two inner numbers to get the outer number.**

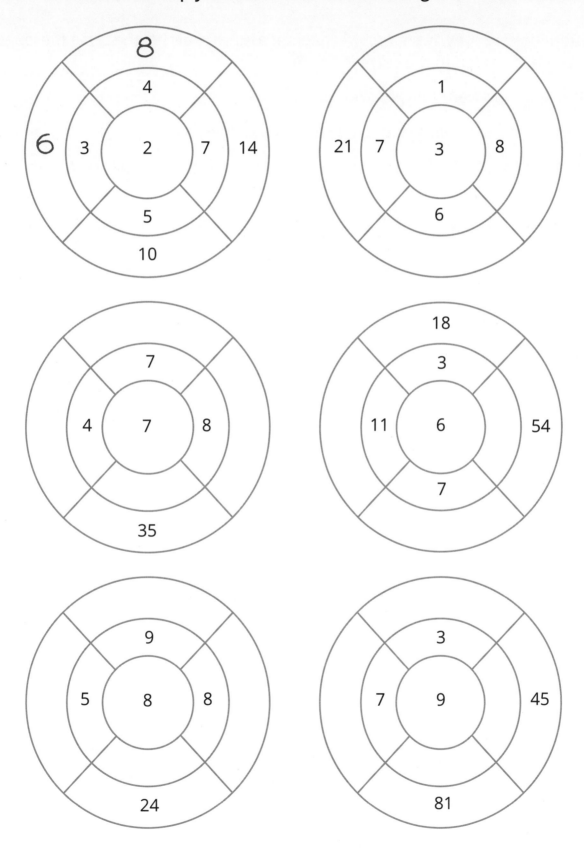

**Solve the logic puzzle.**

Petra, Jonathan, Gabby, Nate, and Michael measured their heights. Use the clues to match each person to the correct height.

Petra's height and Nate's height are both multiples of 9.

Michael's height and Gabby's height are both multiples of 8.

Jonathan is 1 foot taller than Michael and 1 foot shorter than Nate. *Hint: There are 12 inches in a foot.*

| Height | Petra | Jonathan | Gabby | Nate | Michael |
|--------|-------|----------|-------|------|---------|
| 45 inches | | | | | |
| 48 inches | | | | | |
| 56 inches | | | | | |
| 60 inches | | | | | |
| 72 inches | | | | | |

**Solve each riddle. Fill in the missing number.**

If you multiply 5 by the number ___9___, you get 4 less than 7 × 7.

If you multiply 8 by the number _____, you get a number between 3 × 5 and 4 × 5.

The number _____ is a multiple of 9. It is less than 90, and its second digit is twice as big as its first digit.

If you multiply 5 by the number _____ and then again by 4, you get 5 × 8.

**Warm up! Solve these problems.**

$4 \times 27 = \underline{4} \times (\underline{20} + \underline{7})$

$4 \times 27 = (\underline{4} \times \underline{20}) + (\underline{4} \times \underline{7})$

$4 \times 27 = \underline{80} + \underline{28}$

$4 \times 27 = \underline{108}$

$3 \times 35 = \underline{\hspace{1cm}} \times (\underline{\hspace{1cm}} + \underline{\hspace{1cm}})$

$3 \times 35 = (\underline{\hspace{1cm}} \times \underline{\hspace{1cm}}) + (\underline{\hspace{1cm}} \times \underline{\hspace{1cm}})$

$3 \times 35 = \underline{\hspace{1cm}} + \underline{\hspace{1cm}}$

$3 \times 35 = \underline{\hspace{1cm}}$

$4 \times 76 = \underline{\hspace{1cm}} \times (\underline{\hspace{1cm}} + \underline{\hspace{1cm}})$

$4 \times 76 = (\underline{\hspace{1cm}} \times \underline{\hspace{1cm}}) + (\underline{\hspace{1cm}} \times \underline{\hspace{1cm}})$

$4 \times 76 = \underline{\hspace{1cm}} + \underline{\hspace{1cm}}$

$4 \times 76 = \underline{\hspace{1cm}}$

$6 \times 82 = \underline{\hspace{1cm}} \times (\underline{\hspace{1cm}} + \underline{\hspace{1cm}})$

$6 \times 82 = (\underline{\hspace{1cm}} \times \underline{\hspace{1cm}}) + (\underline{\hspace{1cm}} \times \underline{\hspace{1cm}})$

$6 \times 82 = \underline{\hspace{1cm}} + \underline{\hspace{1cm}}$

$6 \times 82 = \underline{\hspace{1cm}}$

**Keep going! Can you solve these in your head?**

$3 \times 34 = \underline{\hspace{1cm}}$

$4 \times 65 = \underline{\hspace{1cm}}$

$5 \times 37 = \underline{\hspace{1cm}}$

$7 \times 58 = \underline{\hspace{1cm}}$

$6 \times 75 = \underline{\hspace{1cm}}$

$9 \times 86 = \underline{\hspace{1cm}}$

## EXPONENTS

You can use a small number called an **exponent** to show perfect squares. For example, in $4^2$, the exponent $2$ means that you multiply two 4s.

$$4^2 = 4 \times 4$$

In $4^3$, the exponent $3$ means that you multiply three 4s.

$$4^3 = 4 \times 4 \times 4$$

You can keep going with other exponents, too!

$$4^4 = 4 \times 4 \times 4 \times 4$$

If you see $4^2$, you can say "4 squared" or "4 to the 2nd power."
For $4^3$, you can say "4 cubed" or "4 to the 3rd power."

### TRY IT YOURSELF!

Match each exponent to what it means.

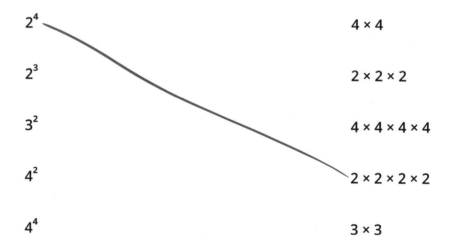

| | |
|---|---|
| $2^4$ | $4 \times 4$ |
| $2^3$ | $2 \times 2 \times 2$ |
| $3^2$ | $4 \times 4 \times 4 \times 4$ |
| $4^2$ | $2 \times 2 \times 2 \times 2$ |
| $4^4$ | $3 \times 3$ |

# EXPONENTS WITH 10

Look at the table. What pattern do you notice?

| Exponents with 10 | | | |
|---|---|---|---|
| $10^2$ | 100 | 2 zeros | hundred |
| $10^3$ | 1,000 | 3 zeros | thousand |
| $10^6$ | 1,000,000 | 6 zeros | million |
| $10^9$ | 1,000,000,000 | 9 zeros | billion |
| $10^{12}$ | 1,000,000,000,000 | 12 zeros | trillion |

## TRY IT YOURSELF!

Write out each number below.

$10^{16}$ = _____

$10^{19}$ = _____

$10^{21}$ = _____

**Multiply.**

3 × 2 × 5 = _____          4 × 3 × 4 = _____

6 × 5 × 2 = _____          2 × 7 × 5 = _____

5 × 3 × 8 = _____          4 × 3 × 6 = _____

**Answer each question.**

Amy wants to put 6 posters on the walls of her room. Each poster is 2 feet wide and 3 feet tall. How much space will the posters take up?

_____ square feet

A box of chocolates has 4 different flavors, with 8 pieces of each flavor. How many pieces of chocolate are in 3 boxes?

_____ pieces

A small theater has 10 rows with 6 seats in each row. Each ticket costs $7. How much money can the theater make in ticket sales for each show?

_____

IXL.com
skill ID
X9H

**Multiply.**

```
   53          54          65
 ×  2        ×  3        ×  4
```

```
   48          29          38
 ×  3        ×  6        ×  7
```

```
   73          69         426
 ×  6        ×  6        ×   5
```

```
  534         475         677
 ×   6       ×   7       ×   8
```

```
  739         486         875
 ×   6       ×   7       ×   8
```

**Answer each question.**

Mariah went to the store and bought 3 loaves of bread and 2 jars of peanut butter. Each loaf of bread was $3, and each jar of peanut butter was $5. If Mariah had $25, how much money was left over?

_____

Harrison has 6 dimes and 5 nickels. How many more nickels does he need to make $1?

_____ nickels

Carol's Café has 7 small tables and 8 large tables. If the small tables have 2 chairs and the large tables have 4 chairs, how many chairs are there in all?

_____ chairs

The swim team is going to a meet across town. They are taking 4 cars and 5 vans. There are 4 people in each car and 7 people in each van. How many people are going to the meet?

_____ people

For a class competition, Tucker wants to read 300 pages by next week. If he reads 4 books that are 70 pages long, will that be enough? If not, how many more pages will he need?

IXL.com
skill ID
**SRL**

**Answer each question.**

Bailey wants to save $120. She earns $8 every hour for babysitting. If she babysits for 9 hours this week, how much more money will she need to earn?

_____

The Ramirez family went to the art museum last week. They bought 5 museum tickets for $9 each. They also bought 5 postcards in the museum gift shop. If the postcards cost $3 each, how much money did the Ramirez family spend in all?

_____

Mr. Duncan is planning the Watsonville Pancake Breakfast. He needs enough pancake mix for 60 people. Each box of pancake mix makes 20 pancakes. Mr. Duncan thinks each person will eat 4 pancakes. How many boxes should Mr. Duncan buy?

_____ boxes

Jaden feeds his cat 2 scoops of food twice a day. There are about 280 scoops in a bag of food. How many weeks will the food last?

_____ weeks

**Find the area of each shaded region.**

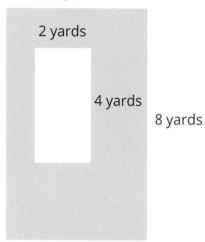

5 yards

2 yards

4 yards

8 yards

__40__ − __8__ = __32__ square yards

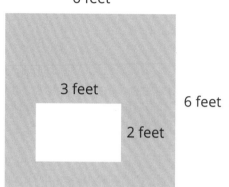

6 feet

3 feet

6 feet

2 feet

_____ − _____ = _____ square feet

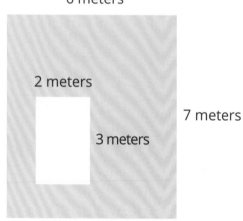

6 meters

2 meters

7 meters

3 meters

_____ − _____ = _____ square meters

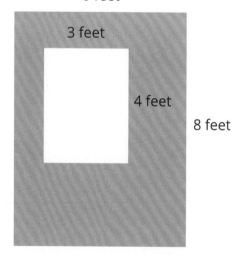

6 feet

3 feet

4 feet

8 feet

_____ − _____ = _____ square feet

# Answer key

**PAGE 2**

2   4   6   8   10  12  14  16  18  20

2   4   6   8   10  12

3   6   9   12  15  18

5   10  15  20  25  30

**PAGE 3**

$2 + 2 + 2 = 6$
3 groups of 2 = 6
$3 \times 2 = 6$

$3 + 3 + 3 = 9$
3 groups of 3 = 9
$3 \times 3 = 9$

$3 + 3 + 3 + 3 = 12$
4 groups of 3 = 12
$4 \times 3 = 12$

$4 + 4 + 4 = 12$
3 groups of 4 = 12
$3 \times 4 = 12$

$2 + 2 + 2 + 2 + 2 = 10$
5 groups of 2 = 10
$5 \times 2 = 10$

$3 + 3 + 3 + 3 + 3 = 15$
5 groups of 3 = 15
$5 \times 3 = 15$

**PAGE 4**

$2 + 2 + 2 = 6$
3 groups of 2 = 6
$3 \times 2 = 6$

$3 + 3 + 3 = 9$
3 groups of 3 = 9
$3 \times 3 = 9$

$3 + 3 + 3 + 3 = 12$
4 groups of 3 = 12
$4 \times 3 = 12$

**PAGE 5**

2 rows of 3 = 6     3 rows of 2 = 6
$2 \times 3 = 6$       $3 \times 2 = 6$

2 rows of 4 = 8     3 rows of 4 = 12
$2 \times 4 = 8$       $3 \times 4 = 12$

4 rows of 1 = 4     4 rows of 4 = 16
$4 \times 1 = 4$       $4 \times 4 = 16$

No. The total is the same.

**PAGE 6**

2 rows of 3 = 6     4 rows of 3 = 12
$2 \times 3 = 6$       $4 \times 3 = 12$

2 rows of 6 = 12    4 rows of 6 = 24
$2 \times 6 = 12$     $4 \times 6 = 24$

**PAGE 7**

3 rows of 5 = 15
$3 \times 5 = 15$

2 groups of 3 = 6
$2 \times 3 = 6$

3 bunches of 4 = 12
$3 \times 4 = 12$

**PAGE 8**

The number 6 is the product. The numbers 2 and 3 are the factors.

$2 \times 4 = 8$      The product is 8.

$3 \times 4 = 12$    The missing factor is 4.

*Answers may vary. One possible answer is shown below.*

$3 \times 3 = 9$

**PAGE 9**

| Batches of cupcakes | Batches × eggs per batch | Total number of eggs |
|---|---|---|
| 1 | $1 \times 2$ | 2 |
| 2 | $2 \times 2$ | 4 |
| 3 | $3 \times 2$ | 6 |
| 4 | $4 \times 2$ | 8 |
| 5 | $5 \times 2$ | 10 |
| 6 | $6 \times 2$ | 12 |
| 7 | $7 \times 2$ | 14 |
| 8 | $8 \times 2$ | 16 |
| 9 | $9 \times 2$ | 18 |
| 10 | $10 \times 2$ | 20 |

All multiples of 2 are even numbers.

**PAGE 10**

$2 \times 4 = 8$      $2 \times 9 = 18$

$2 \times 3 = 6$      $10 \times 2 = 20$

$2 \times 2 = 4$      $5 \times 2 = 10$

$6 \times 2 = 12$     $2 \times 8 = 16$

$4 \times 2 = 8$      $3 \times 2 = 6$

$2 \times 10 = 20$    $2 \times 6 = 12$

$2 \times 7 = 14$     $9 \times 2 = 18$

$2 \times 1 = 2$      $2 \times 5 = 10$

$7 \times 2 = 14$     $2 \times 2 = 4$

$1 \times 2 = 2$      $8 \times 2 = 16$

**PAGE 11**

70   204   558   5,442   100,332,438

1   18   8   12

**PAGE 12**

$3 \times 1 = 3$      $3 \times 6 = 18$

$3 \times 2 = 6$      $3 \times 7 = 21$

$3 \times 3 = 9$      $3 \times 8 = 24$

$3 \times 4 = 12$     $3 \times 9 = 27$

$3 \times 5 = 15$     $3 \times 10 = 30$

The digits of each number add up to a multiple of 3.

**PAGE 13**

63   84   105   372

12   15   24

**PAGE 14**

$3 \times 5 = 15$     $3 \times 10 = 30$

$2 \times 3 = 6$      $4 \times 3 = 12$

$3 \times 6 = 18$     $5 \times 3 = 15$

$3 \times 9 = 27$     $3 \times 4 = 12$

$10 \times 3 = 30$    $3 \times 3 = 9$

$3 \times 3 = 9$      $9 \times 3 = 27$

$3 \times 1 = 3$      $1 \times 3 = 3$

$7 \times 3 = 21$     $3 \times 8 = 24$

$8 \times 3 = 24$     $3 \times 2 = 6$

$6 \times 3 = 18$     $3 \times 7 = 21$

**PAGE 15**

$18

8 comic books

6 patches

21 paint brushes

**PAGE 16**

$3 \times 3 = 9$    $2 \times 10 = 20$   $3 \times 9 = 27$

$2 \times 5 = 10$   $3 \times 2 = 6$     $2 \times 6 = 12$

$3 \times 4 = 12$   $3 \times 7 = 21$    $2 \times 9 = 18$

$3 \times 5 = 15$   $2 \times 1 = 2$     $3 \times 10 = 30$

$2 \times 4 = 8$    $3 \times 6 = 18$    $2 \times 7 = 14$

### PAGE 17

| Number of books | Books × cost per book | Total cost |
|---|---|---|
| 1 | 1 × $4 | $4 |
| 2 | 2 × $4 | $8 |
| 3 | 3 × $4 | $12 |
| 4 | 4 × $4 | $16 |
| 5 | 5 × $4 | $20 |
| 6 | 6 × $4 | $24 |
| 7 | 7 × $4 | $28 |
| 8 | 8 × $4 | $32 |
| 9 | 9 × $4 | $36 |
| 10 | 10 × $4 | $40 |

They are all even because they are also multiples of 2.

### PAGE 18

4 × 2 = 8      4 × 5 = 20      4 × 6 = 24

10 × 4 = 40      1 × 4 = 4      4 × 10 = 40

4 × 4 = 16      3 × 4 = 12      4 × 1 = 4

4 × 3 = 12      4 × 8 = 32      2 × 4 = 8

5 × 4 = 20      9 × 4 = 36      4 × 7 = 28

8 × 4 = 32      4 × 4 = 16      4 × 9 = 36

7 × 4 = 28      6 × 4 = 24      4 × 8 = 32

### PAGE 19

12      20      7

Aaron's favorite number is 8.

Ethan's favorite number is 20.

Mia's favorite number is 4.

Logan's favorite number is 5.

Grace's favorite number is 12.

### PAGE 20

5 × 5 = 25      3 × 5 = 15

2 × 5 = 10      5 × 7 = 35

5 × 1 = 5      9 × 5 = 45

4 × 5 = 20      1 × 5 = 5

7 × 5 = 35      10 × 5 = 50

5 × 9 = 45      5 × 5 = 25

5 × 6 = 30      5 × 8 = 40

5 × 3 = 15      5 × 2 = 10

6 × 5 = 30      5 × 4 = 20

5 × 10 = 50      8 × 5 = 40

All of the multiples of 5 end in 0 or 5.

### PAGE 21

8 × 5 cents = 40 cents

10 × 5 yen = 50 yen

5 × 5 rupees = 25 rupees

9 × 5 pence = 45 pence

### PAGE 22

90      355      4,230      759,205

4 × 8 = 32      5 × 2 = 10      4 × 3 = 12

5 × 6 = 30      7 × 4 = 28      5 × 9 = 45

1 × 5 = 5      4 × 4 = 16      5 × 3 = 15

4 × 5 = 20      8 × 5 = 40      10 × 5 = 50

4 × 2 = 8      9 × 4 = 36      5 × 7 = 35

### PAGE 23

10 players

20 chapters

6 bills

### PAGE 24

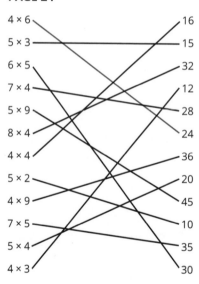

4 × 6      16
5 × 3      15
6 × 5      32
7 × 4      12
5 × 9      28
8 × 4      24
4 × 4      36
5 × 2      20
4 × 9      45
7 × 5      10
5 × 4      35
4 × 3      30

### PAGE 25

2 × 4 = 8      5 × 1 = 5

3 × 6 = 18      7 × 4 = 28

5 × 7 = 35      2 × 6 = 12

8 × 2 = 16      3 × 8 = 24

4 × 4 = 16      9 × 2 = 18

3 × 4 = 12      5 × 2 = 10

5 × 9 = 45      3 × 9 = 27

10 × 3 = 30      4 × 5 = 20

1 × 4 = 4      3 × 3 = 9

5 × 5 = 25      7 × 2 = 14

### PAGE 26

$8

3 mugs

2 mugs

$36

4 frames

### PAGE 27

3 × 5 = 15      3 × 7 = 21      2 × 1 = 2

10 × 2 = 20      8 × 4 = 32      4 × 3 = 12

4 × 6 = 24      5 × 10 = 50      10 × 4 = 40

5 × 6 = 30      3 × 2 = 6      2 × 2 = 4

9 × 4 = 36      8 × 5 = 40      4 × 5 = 20

2 × 9 = 18      4 × 4 = 16      3 × 8 = 24

### PAGE 28

| | | START ↓ | | | |
|---|---|---|---|---|---|
| 4 × 6 | 3 × 3 | 2 × 1 | 1 × 4 | 3 × 4 | 4 × 7 |
| 6 × 5 | 6 × 2 | 4 × 4 | 2 × 7 | 5 × 3 | 6 × 1 |
| 5 × 2 | 4 × 3 | 1 × 3 | 5 × 3 | 2 × 2 | 1 × 2 |
| 4 × 1 | 5 × 2 | 3 × 3 | 3 × 4 | 4 × 1 | 4 × 3 |
| 2 × 2 | 4 × 6 | 4 × 2 | 1 × 5 | 2 × 6 | 5 × 5 |
| | | | FINISH ↓ | | |

### PAGE 29

30 times

32 bars

40 minutes

Yes. He needs only $18.

Tara paid $20. Lisa paid $18. So, Tara paid $2 more than Lisa.

### PAGE 30

You can multiply the factors in any order. You still get the same product.

3 × 7 = 21      4 × 6 = 24

7 × 3 = 21      6 × 4 = 24

5 × 8 = 40      3 × 9 = 27

8 × 5 = 40      9 × 3 = 27

4 × 8 = 32      5 × 6 = 30

8 × 4 = 32      6 × 5 = 30

### PAGE 31

6 × 1 = 6      6 × 6 = 36

6 × 2 = 12      6 × 7 = 42

6 × 3 = 18      6 × 8 = 48

6 × 4 = 24      6 × 9 = 54

6 × 5 = 30      6 × 10 = 60

Each multiple of 6 is also a multiple of 2 and 3.

## PAGE 32

90    1,152    14,580    10,450,236
3 million

The missing digit is 4.

The missing digit could be 1, 4, or 7.

The missing digit could be 2, 5, or 8.

## PAGE 33

| | |
|---|---|
| 6 × 4 = 24 | 8 × 6 = 48 |
| 6 × 6 = 36 | 6 × 10 = 60 |
| 6 × 8 = 48 | 3 × 6 = 18 |
| 9 × 6 = 54 | 5 × 6 = 30 |
| 4 × 6 = 24 | 6 × 1 = 6 |
| 10 × 6 = 60 | 6 × 9 = 54 |
| 6 × 2 = 12 | 6 × 7 = 42 |
| 6 × 5 = 30 | 6 × 3 = 18 |
| 6 × 6 = 36 | 2 × 6 = 12 |
| 1 × 6 = 6 | 7 × 6 = 42 |

## PAGE 34

| Number of weeks | Weeks × days per week | Total number of days |
|---|---|---|
| 1 | 1 × 7 | 7 |
| 2 | 2 × 7 | 14 |
| 3 | 3 × 7 | 21 |
| 4 | 4 × 7 | 28 |
| 5 | 5 × 7 | 35 |
| 6 | 6 × 7 | 42 |
| 7 | 7 × 7 | 49 |
| 8 | 8 × 7 | 56 |
| 9 | 9 × 7 | 63 |
| 10 | 10 × 7 | 70 |

## PAGE 35

| | |
|---|---|
| 7 × 5 = 35 | 7 × 8 = 56 |
| 3 × 7 = 21 | 7 × 1 = 7 |
| 7 × 4 = 28 | 6 × 7 = 42 |
| 7 × 9 = 63 | 5 × 7 = 35 |
| 4 × 7 = 28 | 7 × 10 = 70 |
| 10 × 7 = 70 | 7 × 7 = 49 |
| 7 × 2 = 14 | 9 × 7 = 63 |
| 8 × 7 = 56 | 7 × 3 = 21 |
| 7 × 6 = 42 | 1 × 7 = 7 |
| 2 × 7 = 14 | 7 × 7 = 49 |

## PAGE 36

21 miles

12 bottles

28 socks

$56

Mr. Weber planted 28 tulips. Mrs. Johnson planted 30 tulips. So, Mrs. Johnson planted more.

## PAGE 37

Allison is 6 years old.

Zoe is 12 years old.

Dave is 13 years old.

Chris is 14 years old.

Sandra is 7 years old.

35    7    2

## PAGE 38

*Answers may vary. Some possible answers are shown below.*

(2 × 3) × 3 = 6 × 3 = 18
2 × (3 × 3) = 2 × 9 = 18

(3 × 2) × 5 = 6 × 5 = 30
3 × (2 × 5) = 3 × 10 = 30

(2 × 2) × 4 = 4 × 4 = 16
2 × (2 × 4) = 2 × 8 = 16

## PAGE 39

*Answers may vary. Some possible answers are shown below.*

(1 × 3) × 2 × 4 = 3 × (2 × 4) = 3 × 8 = 24
1 × 3 × (2 × 4) = (1 × 3) × 8 = 3 × 8 = 24
1 × (3 × 2) × 4 = (1 × 6) × 4 = 6 × 4 = 24

3 × 2 × (2 × 1) = (3 × 2) × 2 = 6 × 2 = 12
(3 × 2) × 2 × 1 = 6 × (2 × 1) = 6 × 2 = 12
3 × (2 × 2) × 1 = 3 × (4 × 1) = 3 × 4 = 12

2 × 3 × 2 = 12
3 × 2 × 3 = 18
3 × 3 × 3 = 27

## PAGE 40

| Number of pies | Pies × slices per pie | Total slices of pie |
|---|---|---|
| 1 | 1 × 8 | 8 |
| 2 | 2 × 8 | 16 |
| 3 | 3 × 8 | 24 |
| 4 | 4 × 8 | 32 |
| 5 | 5 × 8 | 40 |
| 6 | 6 × 8 | 48 |
| 7 | 7 × 8 | 56 |
| 8 | 8 × 8 | 64 |
| 9 | 9 × 8 | 72 |
| 10 | 10 × 8 | 80 |

The last digit forms a pattern of 8, 6, 4, 2, 0. The last digit of 8 × 13 will be 4.

## PAGE 41

| | |
|---|---|
| 8 × 5 = 40 | 8 × 8 = 64 |
| 3 × 8 = 24 | 8 × 1 = 8 |
| 8 × 4 = 32 | 2 × 8 = 16 |
| 8 × 9 = 72 | 5 × 8 = 40 |
| 4 × 8 = 32 | 8 × 10 = 80 |
| 10 × 8 = 80 | 8 × 7 = 56 |
| 8 × 2 = 16 | 9 × 8 = 72 |
| 8 × 8 = 64 | 8 × 3 = 24 |
| 6 × 8 = 48 | 1 × 8 = 8 |
| 7 × 8 = 56 | 8 × 6 = 48 |

## PAGE 42

1,040

5,072

336,024

1,009,008

948,302,048

## PAGE 43

| | |
|---|---|
| 9 × 1 = 9 | 9 × 6 = 54 |
| 9 × 2 = 18 | 9 × 7 = 63 |
| 9 × 3 = 27 | 9 × 8 = 72 |
| 9 × 4 = 36 | 9 × 9 = 81 |
| 9 × 5 = 45 | 9 × 10 = 90 |

The digits of each answer add up to 9!

## PAGE 45

To multiply 9 × 5, lower your fifth finger—your left thumb. There are 4 fingers to the left and 5 to the right, so 9 × 5 = 45.

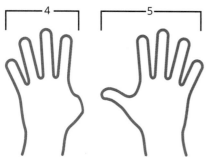

Why does this work? Think about adding 9 to a number. Since 9 is 1 less than 10, adding 9 increases the tens digit by 1 but decreases the ones digit by 1. As you go from finger to finger, you are doing the same thing! The number of fingers to the left increases by 1, and the number of fingers to the right decreases by 1.

## PAGE 46

| | |
|---|---|
| 9 × 4 = 36 | 9 × 7 = 63 |
| 3 × 9 = 27 | 4 × 9 = 36 |
| 6 × 9 = 54 | 5 × 9 = 45 |
| 9 × 1 = 9 | 9 × 6 = 54 |
| 9 × 9 = 81 | 9 × 10 = 90 |
| 10 × 9 = 90 | 9 × 8 = 72 |
| 2 × 9 = 18 | 9 × 9 = 81 |
| 8 × 9 = 72 | 9 × 3 = 27 |
| 9 × 5 = 45 | 9 × 2 = 18 |
| 1 × 9 = 9 | 7 × 9 = 63 |

## PAGE 47

| | | |
|---|---|---|
| 8 × 5 = 40 | 8 × 2 = 16 | 10 × 8 = 80 |
| 9 × 6 = 54 | 9 × 1 = 9 | 3 × 9 = 27 |
| 8 × 4 = 32 | 9 × 5 = 45 | 8 × 8 = 64 |
| 4 × 9 = 36 | 9 × 2 = 18 | 8 × 3 = 24 |
| 9 × 7 = 63 | 8 × 6 = 48 | 9 × 8 = 72 |

## PAGE 48

24 books

$45

9 campers

48 eggs

No. She needs 40 mini muffins.

## PAGE 49

| | |
|---|---|
| 7 × 3 = 21 | 6 × 1 = 6 |
| 4 × 9 = 36 | 4 × 8 = 32 |
| 5 × 6 = 30 | 7 × 9 = 63 |
| 6 × 9 = 54 | 6 × 4 = 24 |
| 8 × 8 = 64 | 5 × 7 = 35 |
| 3 × 9 = 27 | 10 × 8 = 80 |
| 7 × 6 = 42 | 6 × 2 = 12 |
| 2 × 8 = 16 | 7 × 7 = 49 |
| 1 × 9 = 9 | 8 × 6 = 48 |
| 7 × 10 = 70 | 4 × 7 = 28 |

## PAGE 50

$21

The 4 slices of combo pizza cost $36. The 6 slices of cheese pizza cost $30. So, the 4 slices of combo pizza cost more.

Their meal cost $57.

The 4 slices of veggie pizza cost $28. The 4 slices of pepperoni pizza cost $24. So, the 4 slices of veggie pizza cost $4 more.

## PAGE 51

24 concerts

42 points

Yes. She has 28 quarts of paint. She needs only 24 quarts.

Carlos has $40. The posters cost $45. He needs $5 more.

## PAGE 52

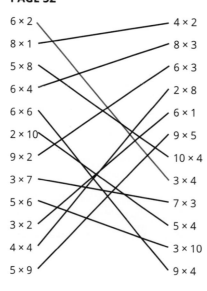

## PAGE 53

| Number of decades | Decades × number of years in a decade | Total number of years |
|---|---|---|
| 1 | 1 × 10 | 10 |
| 2 | 2 × 10 | 20 |
| 3 | 3 × 10 | 30 |
| 4 | 4 × 10 | 40 |
| 5 | 5 × 10 | 50 |
| 6 | 6 × 10 | 60 |
| 7 | 7 × 10 | 70 |
| 8 | 8 × 10 | 80 |
| 9 | 9 × 10 | 90 |
| 10 | 10 × 10 | 100 |

Multiplying by 10 adds a zero to the end of a number. So, 11 × 10 will be 110, and 23 × 10 will be 230.

## PAGE 54

| | |
|---|---|
| 10 × 3 = 30 | 10 × 2 = 20 |
| 6 × 10 = 60 | 1 × 10 = 10 |
| 10 × 8 = 80 | 5 × 10 = 50 |
| 2 × 10 = 20 | 10 × 4 = 40 |
| 9 × 10 = 90 | 10 × 5 = 50 |
| 3 × 10 = 30 | 10 × 7 = 70 |
| 10 × 1 = 10 | 10 × 6 = 60 |
| 7 × 10 = 70 | 10 × 10 = 100 |
| 10 × 10 = 100 | 10 × 9 = 90 |
| 4 × 10 = 40 | 8 × 10 = 80 |

## PAGE 55

| | | |
|---|---|---|
| 160 | 60 | 700 |
| 40,030 | 1 million | 1 trillion |
| $70 | 4 cars | 60 cents |

## PAGE 56

4 × 60 = 240

4 × 600 = 2,400

4 × 6,000 = 24,000

4 × 60,000 = 240,000

4 × 600,000 = 2,400,000

5 × 3,000 = 15,000

2 × 90,000 = 180,000

9 × 60,000 = 540,000

7 × 400,000 = 2,800,000

6 × 700,000 = 4,200,000

8 × 5,000,000 = 40,000,000

## PAGE 57

$600

100,000 gallons

9,000,000 tickets

## PAGE 58

| | |
|---|---|
| 3 × 6 = 18 | 4 × 8 = 32 |
| 9 × 2 = 18 | 6 × 4 = 24 |
| 4 × 4 = 16 | 7 × 9 = 63 |
| 6 × 5 = 30 | 2 × 10 = 20 |
| 10 × 5 = 50 | 7 × 7 = 49 |
| 7 × 3 = 21 | 5 × 5 = 25 |
| 4 × 9 = 36 | 9 × 6 = 54 |
| 3 × 4 = 12 | 5 × 8 = 40 |
| 2 × 8 = 16 | 7 × 6 = 42 |
| 6 × 6 = 36 | 8 × 7 = 56 |

## PAGE 59

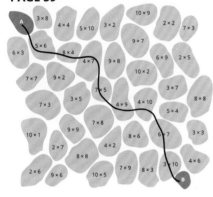

## PAGE 60

10    35    8

Answers may vary. Some possible answers are shown below.

| | |
|---|---|
| 2 × 6 = 12 | 3 × 4 = 12 |
| 4 × 6 = 24 | 8 × 3 = 24 |
| 5 × 8 = 40 | 4 × 10 = 40 |

## PAGE 61

| | | |
|---|---|---|
| 3 × 8 = 24 | 7 × 2 = 14 | 9 × 9 = 81 |
| 6 × 8 = 48 | 2 × 9 = 18 | 10 × 7 = 70 |
| 5 × 4 = 20 | 9 × 5 = 45 | 3 × 5 = 15 |
| 5 × 7 = 35 | 9 × 4 = 36 | 8 × 8 = 64 |
| 3 × 9 = 27 | 9 × 8 = 72 | 8 × 3 = 24 |
| 10 × 6 = 60 | 7 × 7 = 49 | 6 × 9 = 54 |

## PAGE 62

5 × 16 = 5 × (10 + 6)

5 × 16 = (5 × 10) + (5 × 6)

5 × 16 = 50 + 30

5 × 16 = 80

## PAGE 63

*Answers may vary. Some possible answers are shown below.*

7 × 15 = 7 × (10 + 5)

7 × 15 = (7 × 10) + (7 × 5)

7 × 15 = 70 + 35

7 × 15 = 105

4 × 18 = 4 × (10 + 8)

4 × 18 = (4 × 10) + (4 × 8)

4 × 18 = 40 + 32

4 × 18 = 72

8 × 19 = 8 × (10 + 9)

8 × 19 = (8 × 10) + (8 × 9)

8 × 19 = 80 + 72

8 × 19 = 152

## PAGE 64

| | |
|---|---|
| 0 × 1 = 0 | 0 × 6 = 0 |
| 0 × 2 = 0 | 0 × 7 = 0 |
| 0 × 3 = 0 | 0 × 8 = 0 |
| 0 × 4 = 0 | 0 × 9 = 0 |
| 0 × 5 = 0 | 0 × 10 = 0 |

0 × 25 = 0

0 × 4,000,000 = 0

## PAGE 65

| | |
|---|---|
| 1 × 7 = 7 | 3 × 1 = 3 |
| 2 × 1 = 2 | 1 × 5 = 5 |
| 10 × 1 = 10 | 7 × 1 = 7 |
| 1 × 8 = 8 | 1 × 1 = 1 |
| 6 × 1 = 6 | 4 × 1 = 4 |
| 1 × 2 = 2 | 5 × 1 = 5 |
| 1 × 9 = 9 | 1 × 6 = 6 |

1 × 48 = 48

327 × 1 = 327

33,250 × 1 = 33,250

1 × 5,034,150 = 5,034,150

## PAGE 66

| | |
|---|---|
| 11 × 1 = 11 | 11 × 6 = 66 |
| 11 × 2 = 22 | 11 × 7 = 77 |
| 11 × 3 = 33 | 11 × 8 = 88 |
| 11 × 4 = 44 | 11 × 9 = 99 |
| 11 × 5 = 55 | 11 × 10 = 110 |

In each of the first nine products, the tens digits is the same as the ones digit.

## PAGE 67

| Dozens of donuts | Dozens × number of donuts in one dozen | Total number of donuts |
|---|---|---|
| 1 | 1 × 12 | 12 |
| 2 | 2 × 12 | 24 |
| 3 | 3 × 12 | 36 |
| 4 | 4 × 12 | 48 |
| 5 | 5 × 12 | 60 |
| 6 | 6 × 12 | 72 |
| 7 | 7 × 12 | 84 |
| 8 | 8 × 12 | 96 |
| 9 | 9 × 12 | 108 |
| 10 | 10 × 12 | 120 |
| 11 | 11 × 12 | 132 |
| 12 | 12 × 12 | 144 |

The multiples of 12 are also multiples of 2, 3, and 6. They are all even, and their digits add up to multiples of 3. They are also multiples of 4, since 4 is a factor of 12.

## PAGE 68

44 campers

36 inches

48 cookies

33 people

## PAGE 69

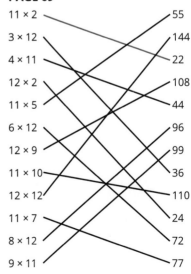

# Answer key

## PAGE 70
2! = 2
3! = 6
4! = 24
7! = 5,040
10! = 3,628,800
12! = 479,001,600

## PAGE 71
3 × 11 = 33    4 × 6 = 24
8 × 8 = 64    12 × 5 = 60
10 × 7 = 70    6 × 9 = 54
6 × 11 = 66    0 × 5 = 0
7 × 8 = 56    3 × 7 = 21
8 × 12 = 96    9 × 1 = 9
5 × 5 = 25    11 × 0 = 0
4 × 8 = 32    12 × 4 = 48
1 × 7 = 7    11 × 12 = 132
5 × 10 = 50    9 × 12 = 108

## PAGE 72
6 × 6 = 36    11 × 2 = 22    9 × 7 = 63
12 × 8 = 96    3 × 6 = 18    12 × 5 = 60
3 × 11 = 33    9 × 6 = 54    7 × 8 = 56
8 × 5 = 40    12 × 4 = 48    8 × 11 = 88
9 × 3 = 27    6 × 7 = 42    7 × 12 = 84

## PAGE 73
56 hot dogs
48 roses
12 cars
11 fish bowls

## PAGE 74
2 × 2 = 4    3 × 3 = 9    4 × 4 = 16

5 × 5 = 25    1 × 1 = 1
6 × 6 = 36    7 × 7 = 49
8 × 8 = 64    9 × 9 = 81

9    25    49
16    36    100

## PAGE 75

1    3    5    7

9    11

You add an odd number to get from one square number to the next. The odd number gets bigger by two each time.

## PAGE 76
14 × 2 = 28    23 × 2 = 46    34 × 2 = 68
73 × 3 = 219    62 × 3 = 186    61 × 5 = 305

## PAGE 77
54 × 2 = 108    42 × 3 = 126    61 × 4 = 244
83 × 3 = 249    81 × 5 = 405    93 × 2 = 186
84 × 2 = 168    92 × 4 = 368    71 × 5 = 355

## PAGE 78
24 × 6 = 144    33 × 5 = 165    26 × 3 = 78
39 × 4 = 156    48 × 7 = 336    72 × 5 = 360

## PAGE 79
43 × 4 = 172    55 × 2 = 110    46 × 3 = 138
54 × 7 = 378    77 × 8 = 616    69 × 5 = 345
67 × 3 = 201    38 × 9 = 342    75 × 6 = 450
94 × 8 = 752    86 × 9 = 774    79 × 7 = 553

## PAGE 80
$88
72 hours
130 students
243 paintings
136 people

## PAGE 81
144 × 2 = 288    232 × 3 = 696    313 × 3 = 939
334 × 2 = 668    421 × 4 = 1,684    501 × 5 = 2,505

## PAGE 82
224 × 3 = 672    246 × 4 = 984    518 × 3 = 1,554

## PAGE 83
469 × 5 = 2,345    522 × 4 = 2,088    935 × 8 = 7,480
443 × 2 = 886    546 × 7 = 3,822    283 × 2 = 566
475 × 5 = 2,375    956 × 6 = 5,736    837 × 7 = 5,859
679 × 7 = 4,753    794 × 8 = 6,352    795 × 9 = 7,155

## PAGE 84
$684
432 cupcakes
$1,700
Yes. The binders can fit 570 baseball cards.
7,668 cartons

## PAGE 85
34 × 2 = 68    63 × 3 = 189    92 × 4 = 368
46 × 3 = 138    55 × 5 = 275    86 × 7 = 602
523 × 3 = 1,569    464 × 4 = 1,856    357 × 5 = 1,785
643 × 7 = 4,501    569 × 7 = 3,983    857 × 9 = 7,713

## PAGE 86
190 grams

585 grams

Yes. You need 210 grams.

72 cookies

## PAGE 87
$162

54 pairs

$486

$1,134

## PAGE 88

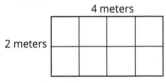

2 × 4 = 8 square meters

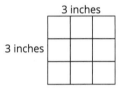

3 × 3 = 9 square inches

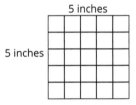

5 × 5 = 25 square inches

2 × 6 = 12 square meters

## PAGE 89
20 square inches     28 square meters

40 square feet     24 square feet

49 square yards     63 square feet

## PAGE 90
6 inches     5 meters

7 yards     7 feet

8 feet     6 feet

## PAGE 91
12 square feet     80 square inches

Grayson's notebook is 24 square inches. Amanda's notebook is 40 square inches. Amanda's notebook is bigger by 16 square inches.

The old tickets were 21 square inches. The new tickets are 12 square inches. They are smaller by 9 square inches.

## PAGE 92
40 square feet

20 square yards

## PAGE 93
36 square feet

57 square meters

59 square feet

## PAGE 94
| | | |
|---|---|---|
| 3 × 6 = 18 | 4 × 5 = 20 | 1 × 12 = 12 |
| 8 × 5 = 40 | 0 × 8 = 0 | 11 × 6 = 66 |
| 7 × 4 = 28 | 3 × 9 = 27 | 6 × 9 = 54 |
| 10 × 7 = 70 | 12 × 4 = 48 | 8 × 7 = 56 |

| | | |
|---|---|---|
| 4 × 4 = 16 | 1 × 9 = 9 | 8 × 6 = 48 |
| 3 × 8 = 24 | 7 × 5 = 35 | 0 × 5 = 0 |
| 7 × 6 = 42 | 4 × 9 = 36 | 5 × 5 = 25 |
| 9 × 11 = 99 | 12 × 5 = 60 | 7 × 9 = 63 |

## PAGE 95

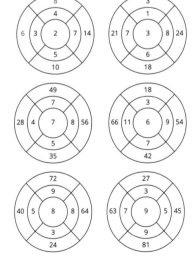

## PAGE 96
Petra is 45 inches tall.

Jonathan is 60 inches tall.

Gabby is 56 inches tall.

Nate is 72 inches tall.

Michael is 48 inches tall.

9    2    36    2

## PAGE 97
*Answers may vary. Some possible answers are shown below.*

4 × 27 = 4 × (20 + 7)

4 × 27 = (4 × 20) + (4 × 7)

4 × 27 = 80 + 28

4 × 27 = 108

3 × 35 = 3 × (30 + 5)

3 × 35 = (3 × 30) + (3 × 5)

3 × 35 = 90 + 15

3 × 35 = 105

4 × 76 = 4 × (70 + 6)

4 × 76 = (4 × 70) + (4 × 6)

4 × 76 = 280 + 24

4 × 76 = 304

6 × 82 = 6 × (80 + 2)

6 × 82 = (6 × 80) + (6 × 2)

6 × 82 = 480 + 12

6 × 82 = 492

3 × 34 = 102     4 × 65 = 260

5 × 37 = 185     7 × 58 = 406

6 × 75 = 450     9 × 86 = 774

## PAGE 98

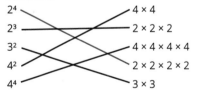

$2^4$

$2^3$

$3^2$

$4^2$

$4^4$

4 × 4

2 × 2 × 2

4 × 4 × 4 × 4

2 × 2 × 2 × 2

3 × 3

## PAGE 99
The number of zeros is the same as the number in the exponent.

$10^{16}$ = 10,000,000,000,000,000

$10^{19}$ = 10,000,000,000,000,000,000

$10^{21}$ = 1,000,000,000,000,000,000,000

**Answer key**

## PAGE 100

$3 \times 2 \times 5 = 30$    $4 \times 3 \times 4 = 48$

$6 \times 5 \times 2 = 60$    $2 \times 7 \times 5 = 70$

$5 \times 3 \times 8 = 120$    $4 \times 3 \times 6 = 72$

36 square feet

96 pieces

$420

## PAGE 101

| | | |
|---|---|---|
| 53 × 2 = 106 | 54 × 3 = 162 | 65 × 4 = 260 |
| 48 × 3 = 144 | 29 × 6 = 174 | 38 × 7 = 266 |
| 73 × 6 = 438 | 69 × 6 = 414 | 426 × 5 = 2,130 |
| 534 × 6 = 3,204 | 475 × 7 = 3,325 | 677 × 8 = 5,416 |
| 739 × 6 = 4,434 | 486 × 7 = 3,402 | 875 × 8 = 7,000 |

## PAGE 102

Mariah spent $19, so she has $6 left over.

He has 85 cents. He needs 15 more cents, or 3 more nickels.

46 chairs

51 people

No. That would be 280 pages. He will need 20 more pages.

## PAGE 103

She will earn $72. So, she will need $48 more.

$60

12 boxes

Jaden feeds his cat 2 scoops of food twice a day, which is 4 scoops of food each day. So, he uses 28 scoops per week. The food will last 10 weeks.

## PAGE 104

40 - 8 = 32 square yards

36 - 6 = 30 square feet

42 - 6 = 36 square meters

48 - 12 = 36 square feet